VICTORIAN FANTASY

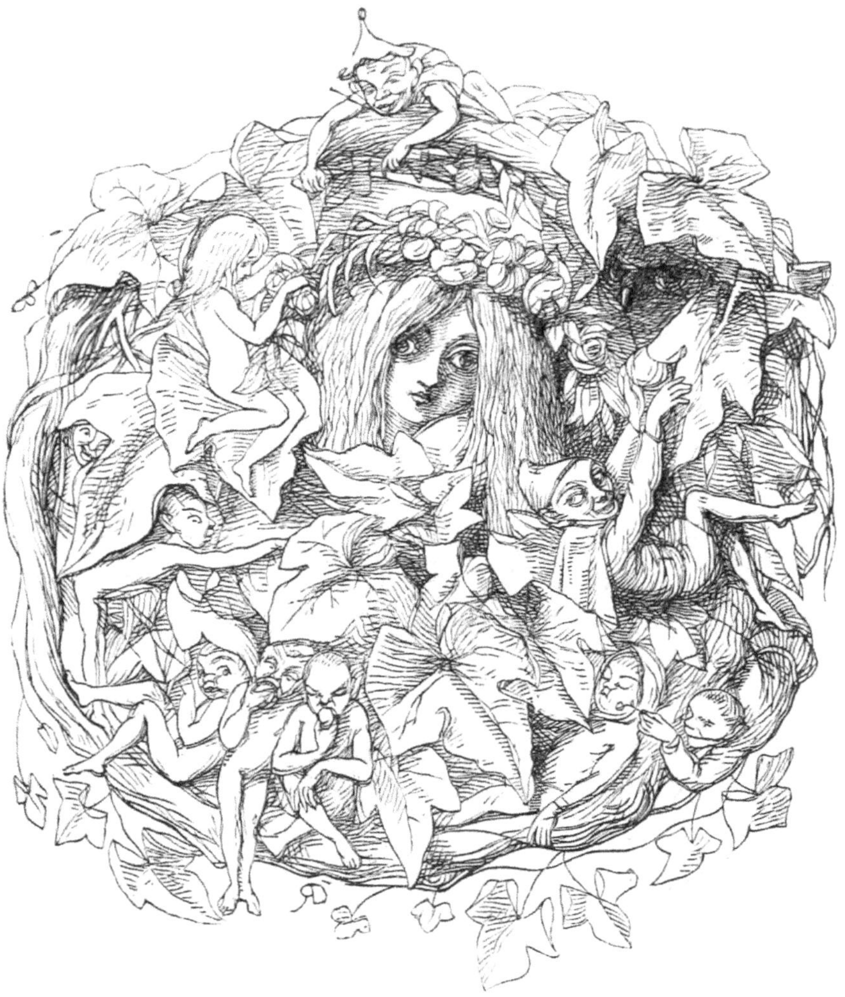

GRAYSCALE ADULT COLORING BOOK

OLDE GLORIE STUDIOS

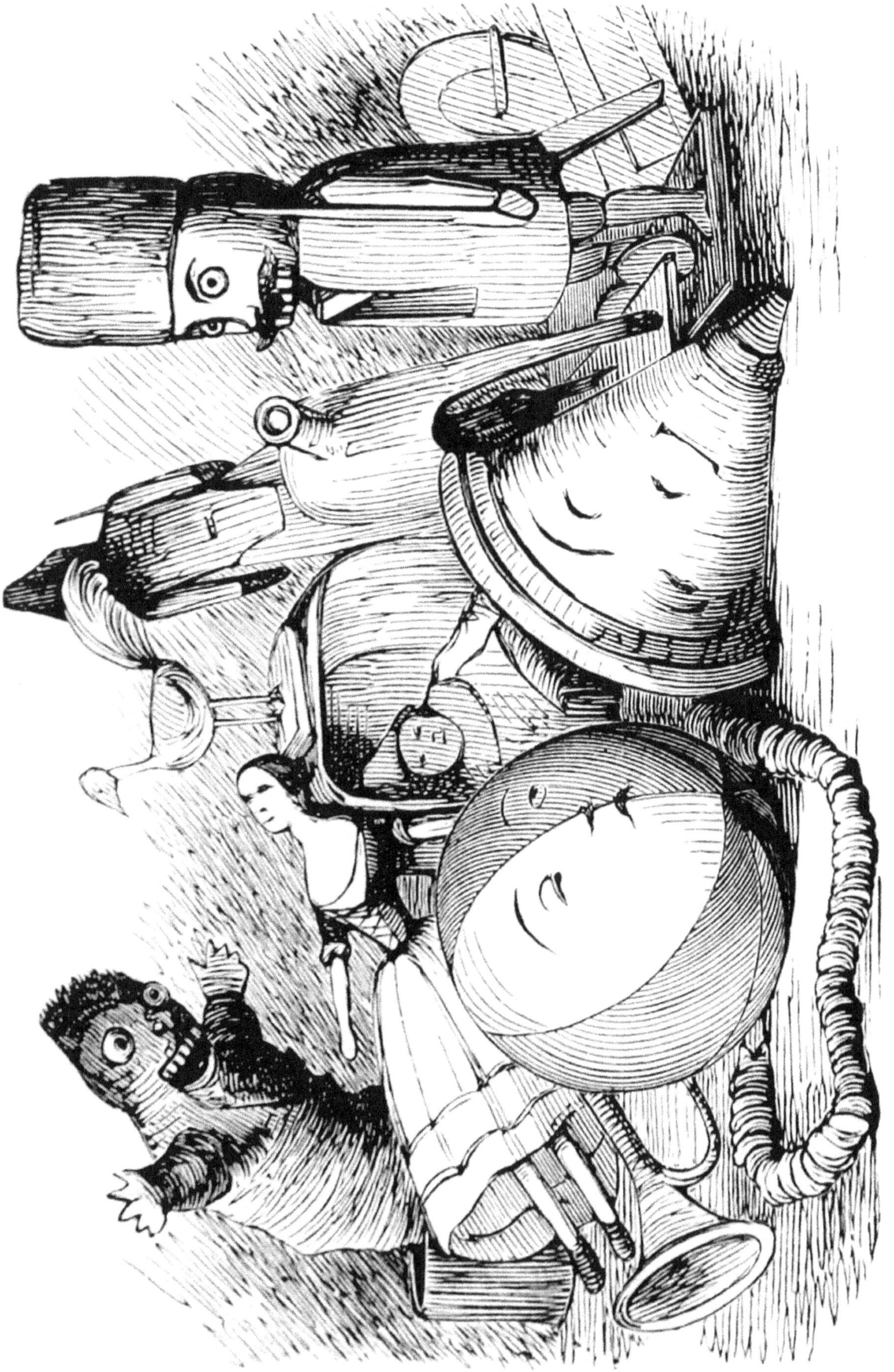

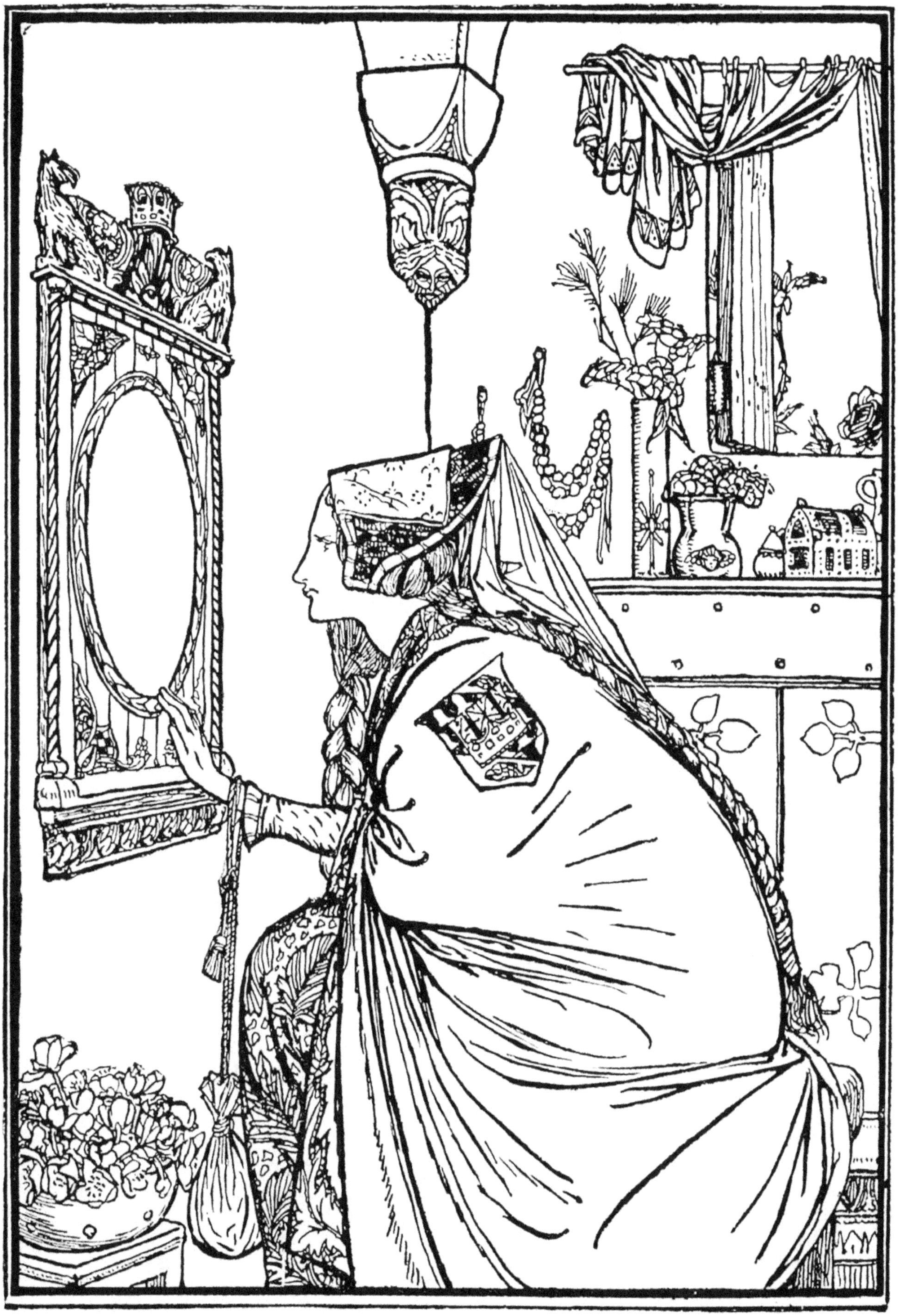

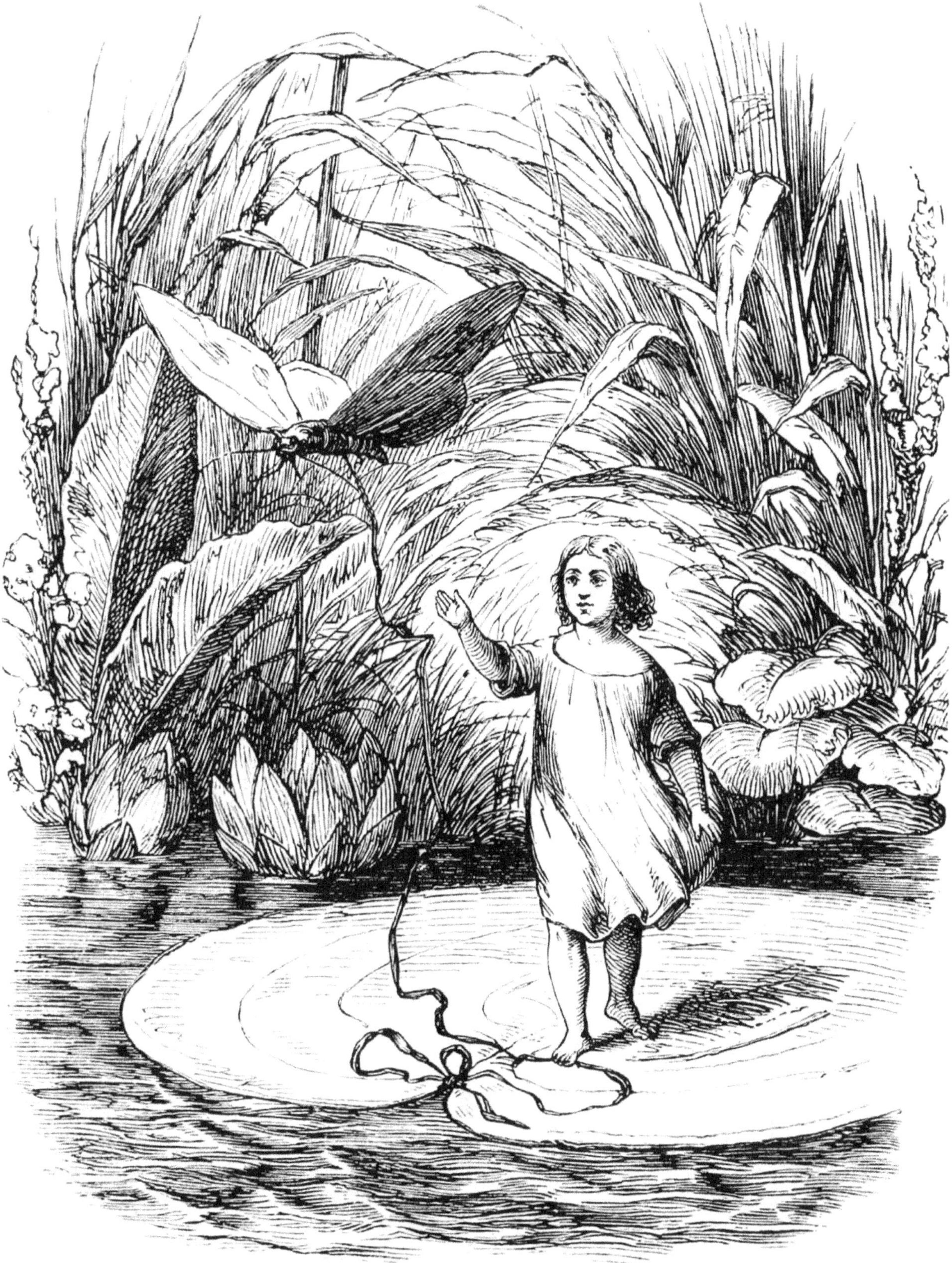

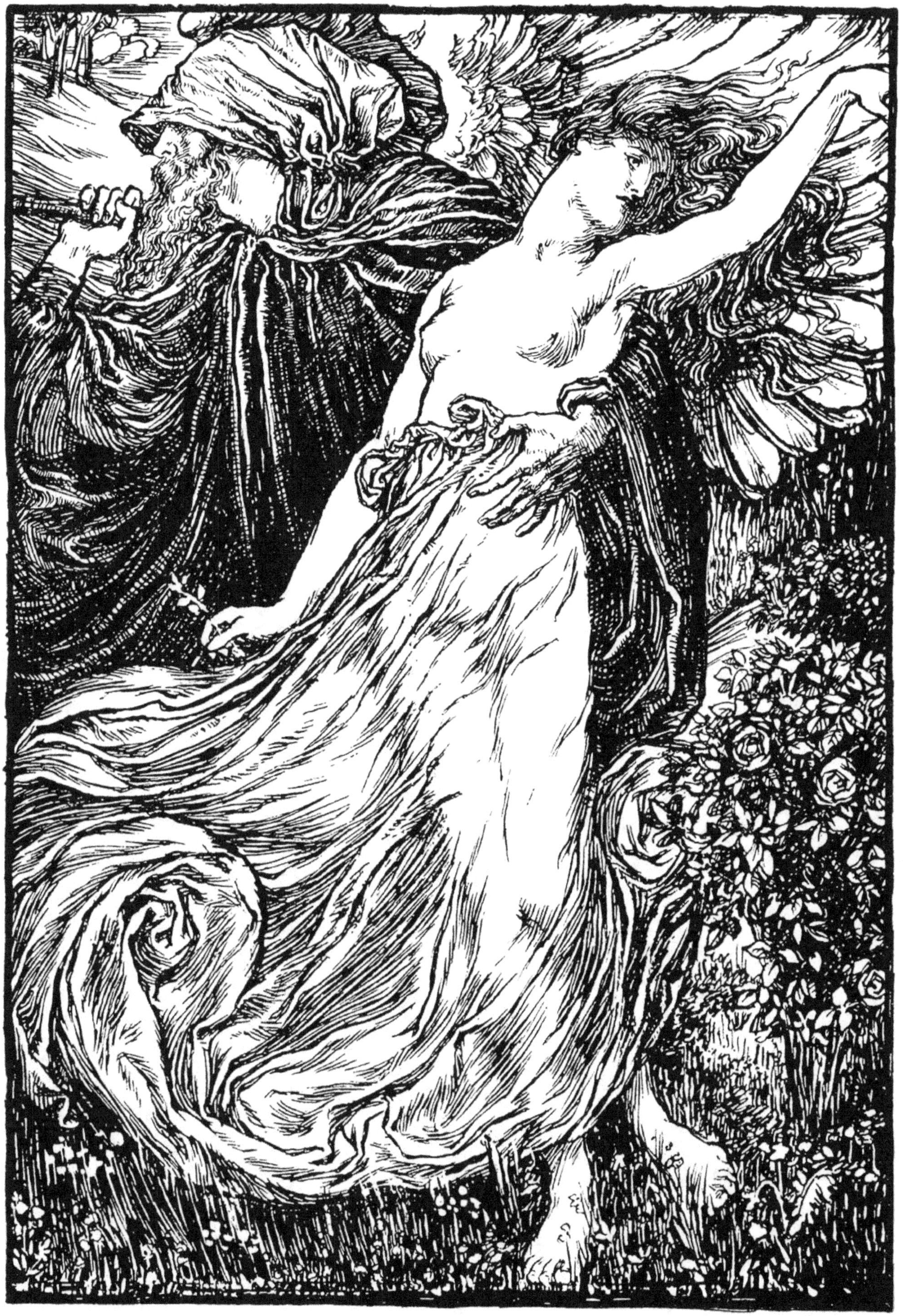

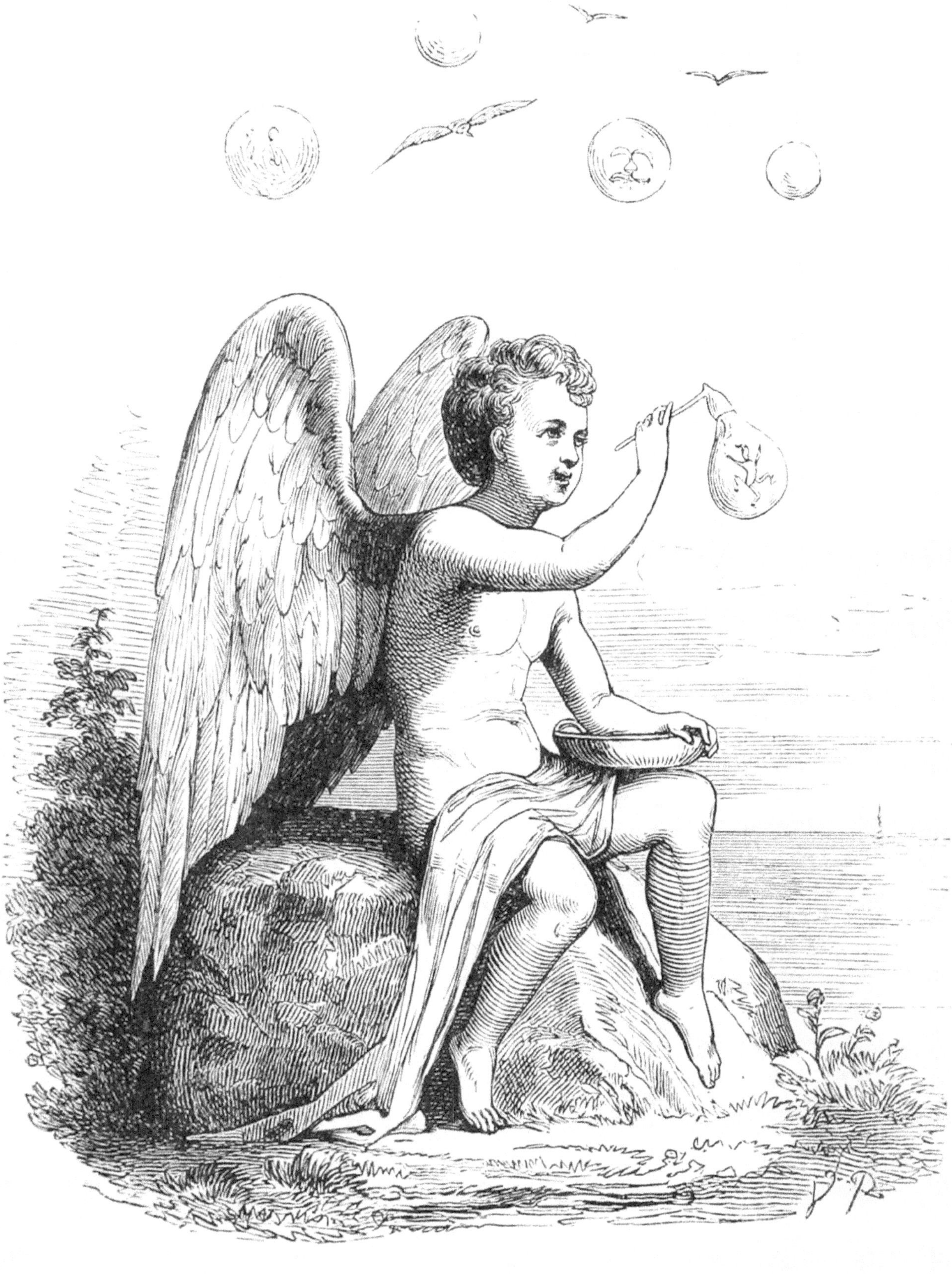

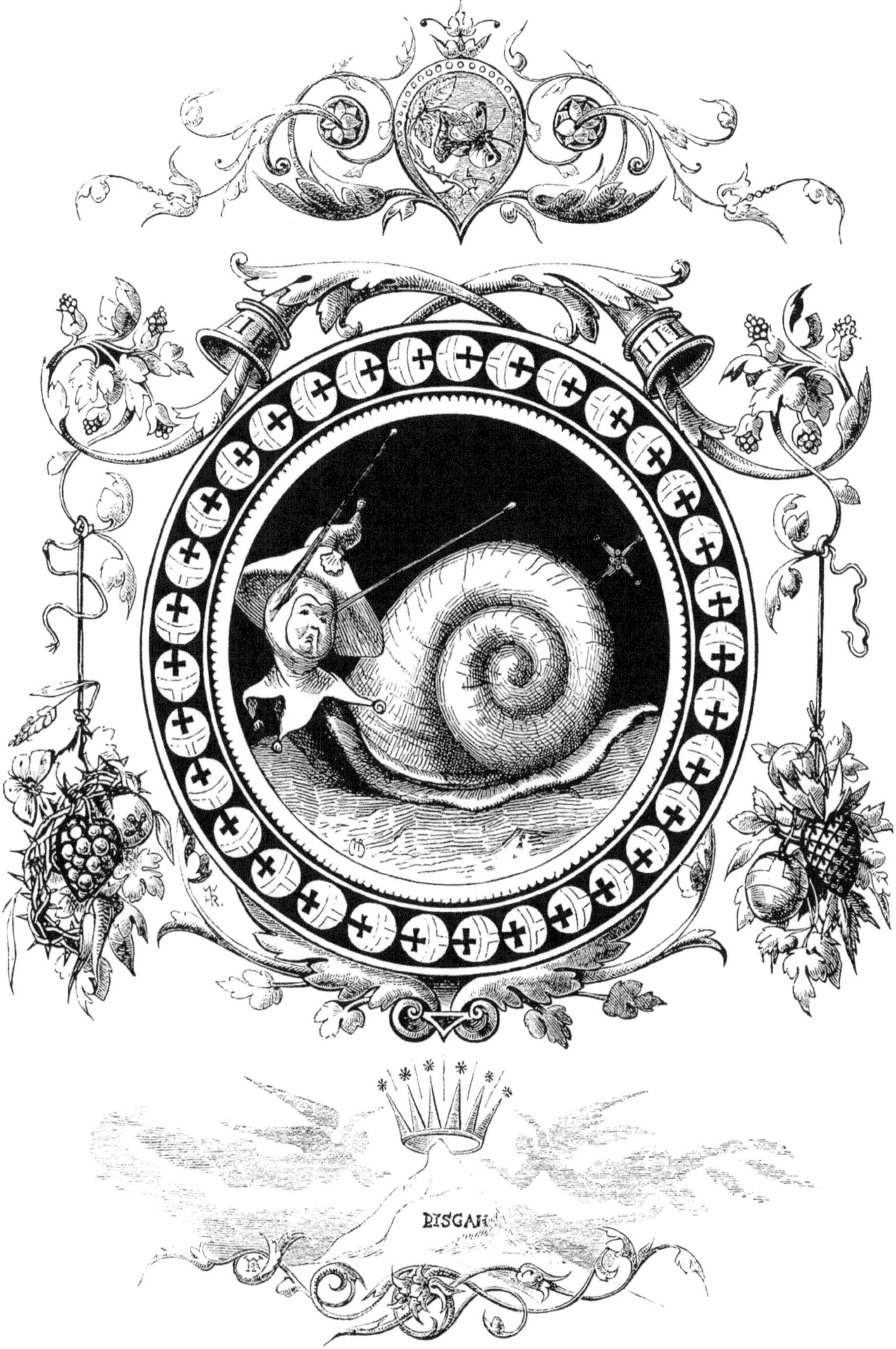
PISGAH

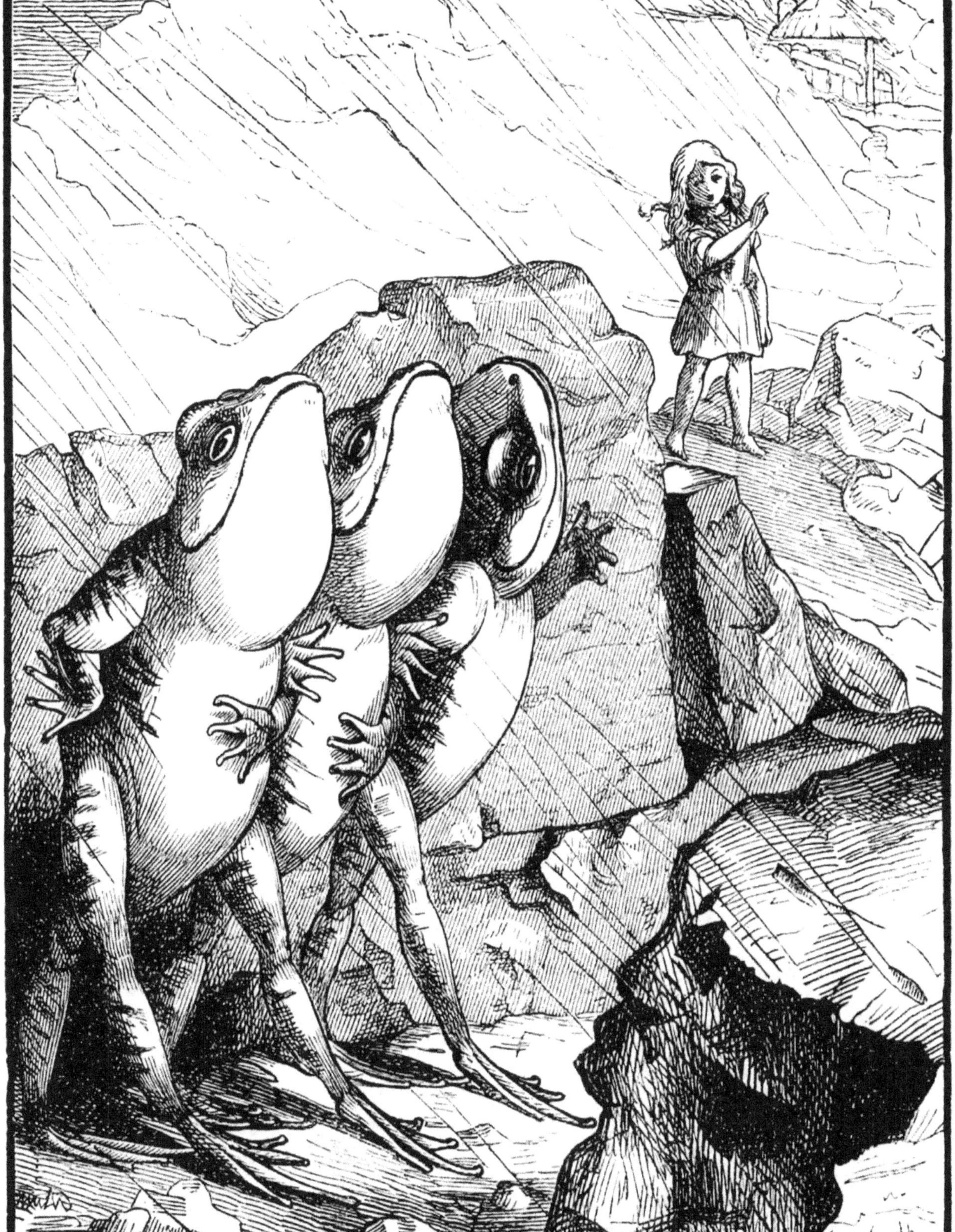

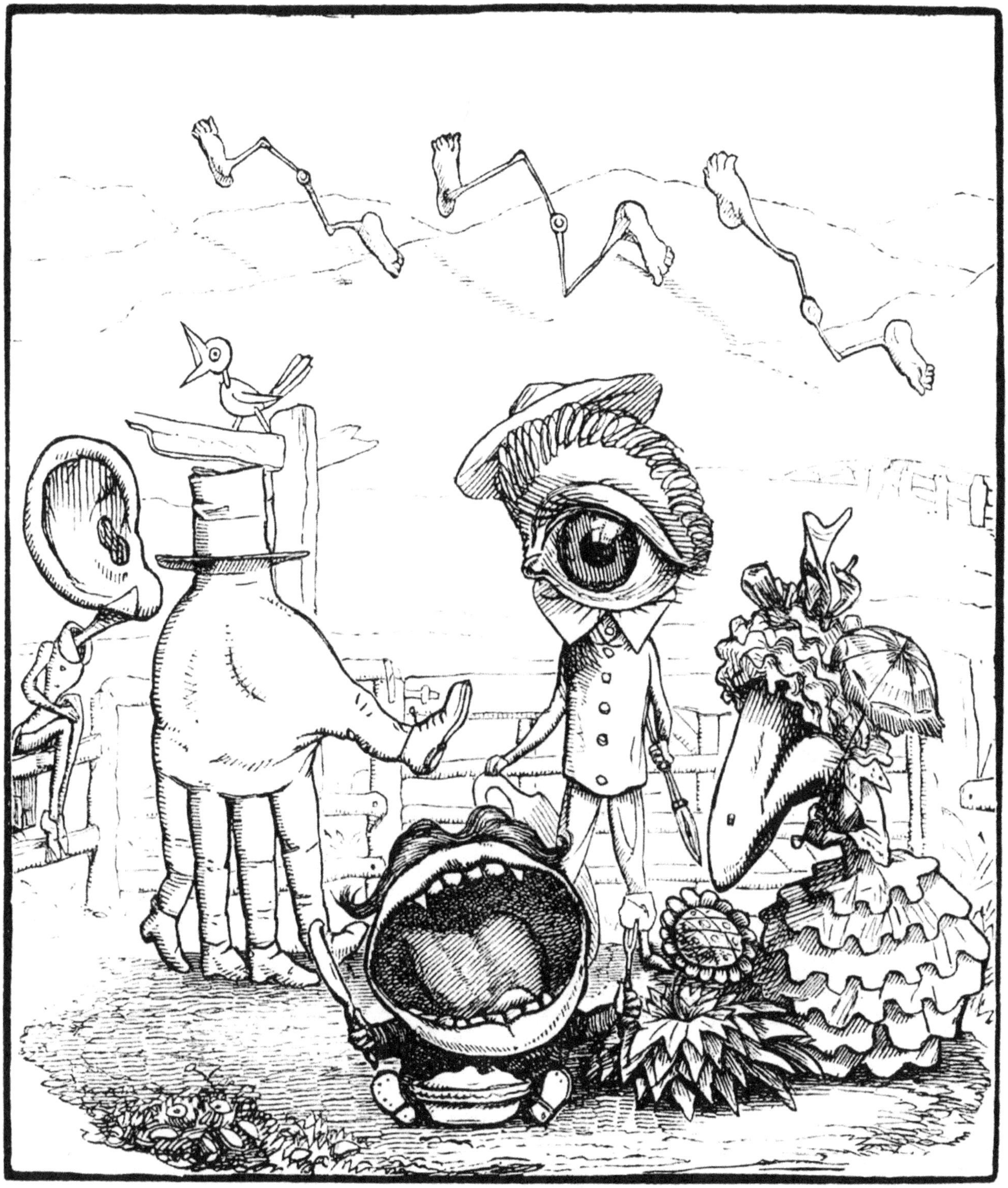

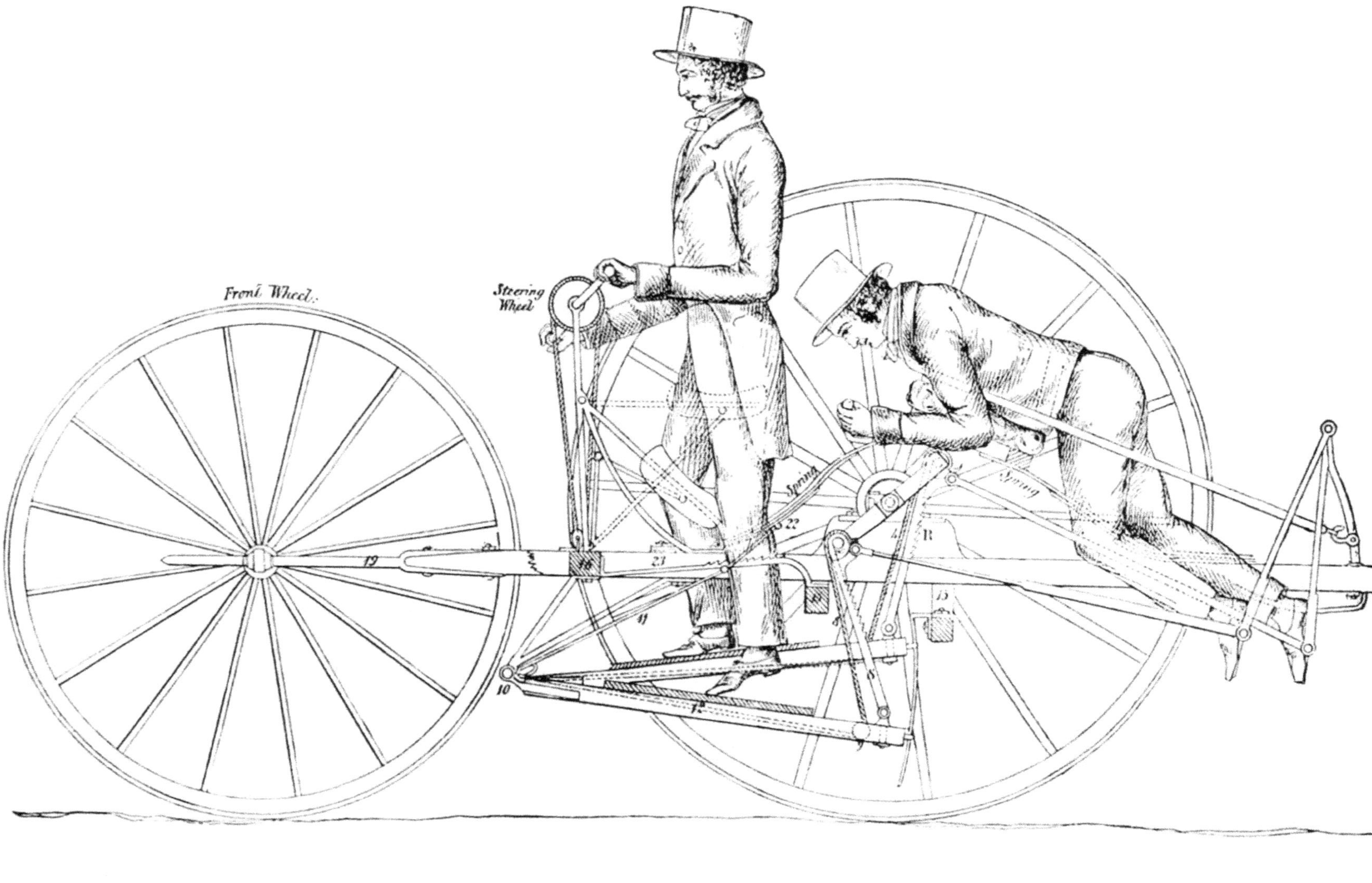
Front Wheel.
Steering Wheel
Spring
Spring

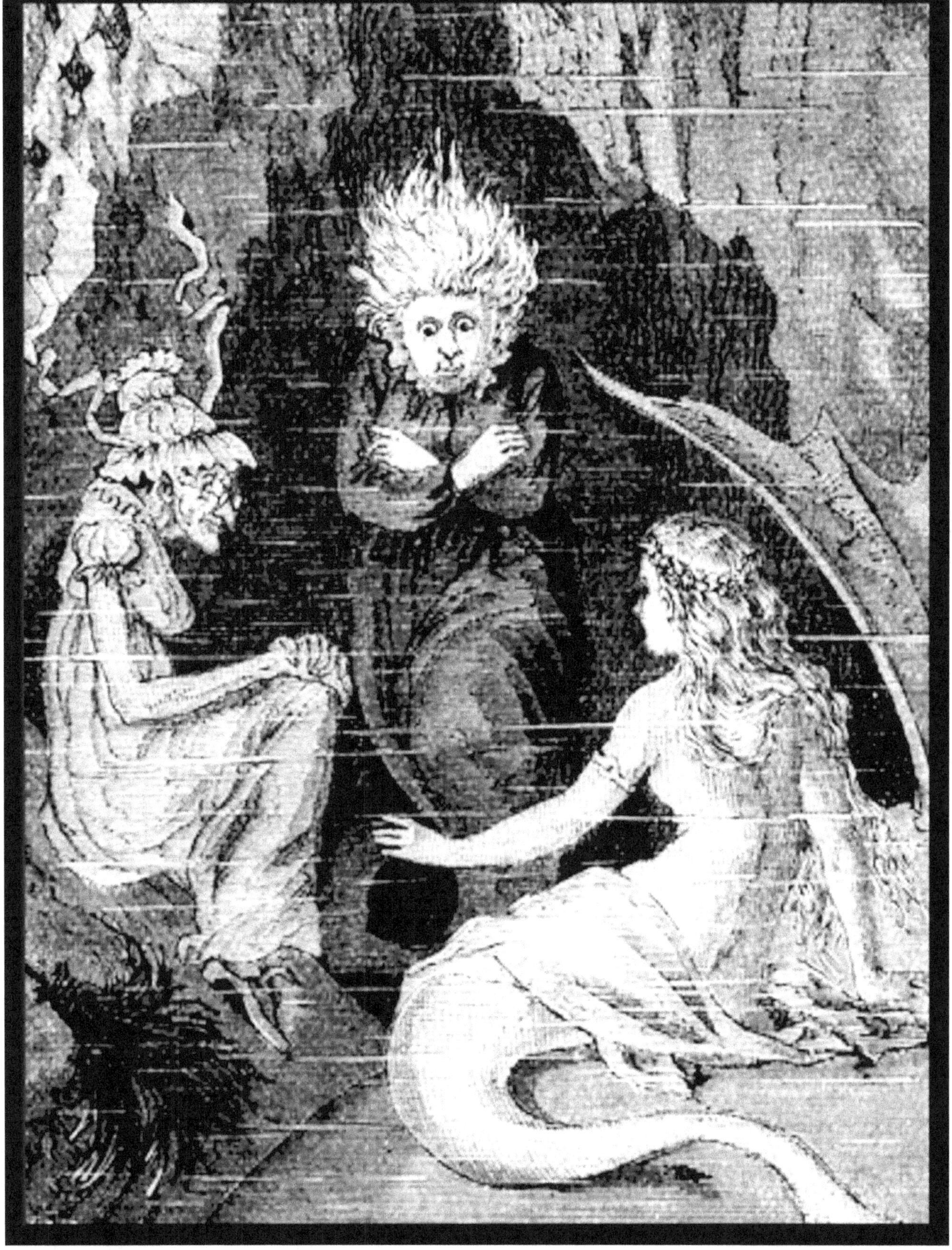

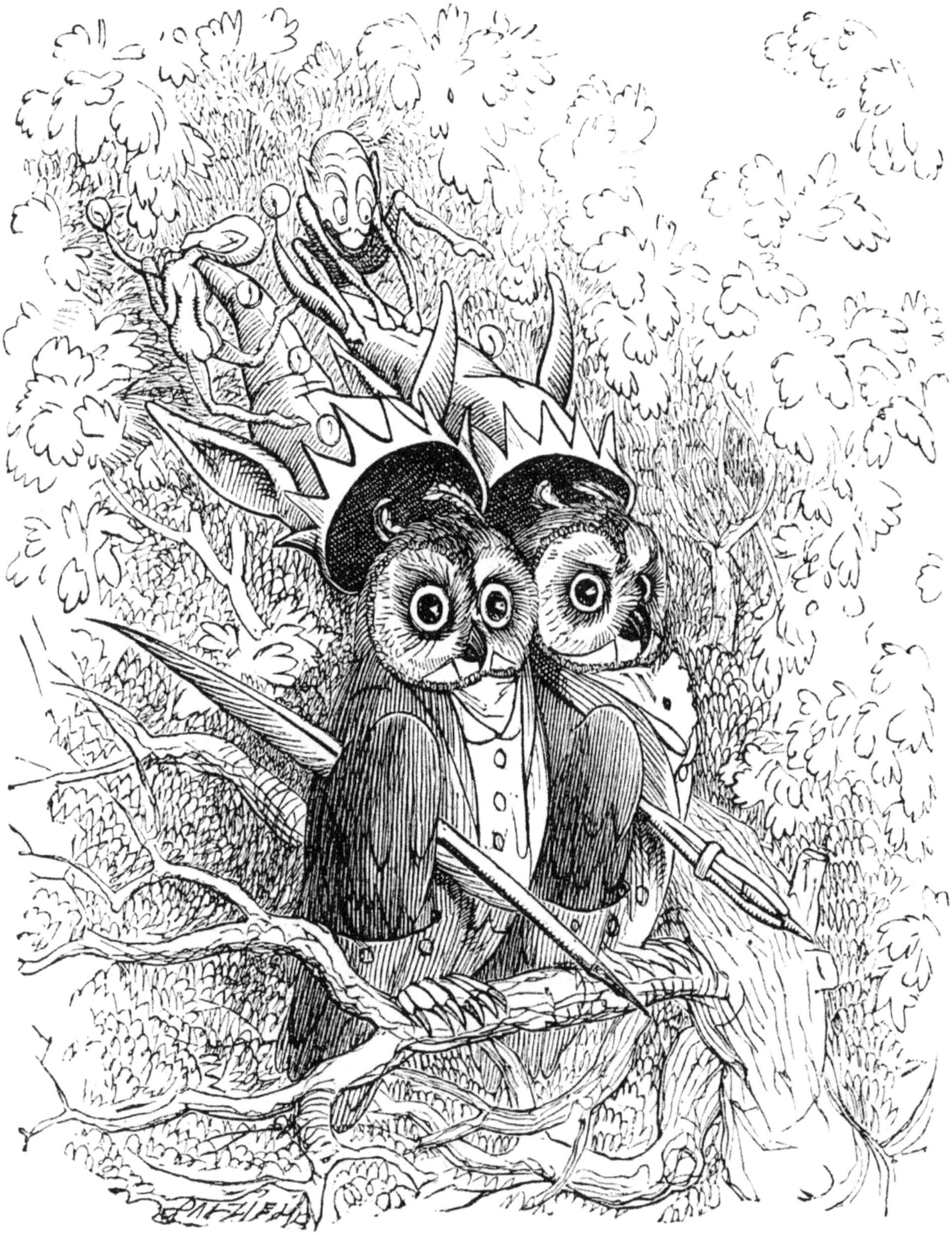

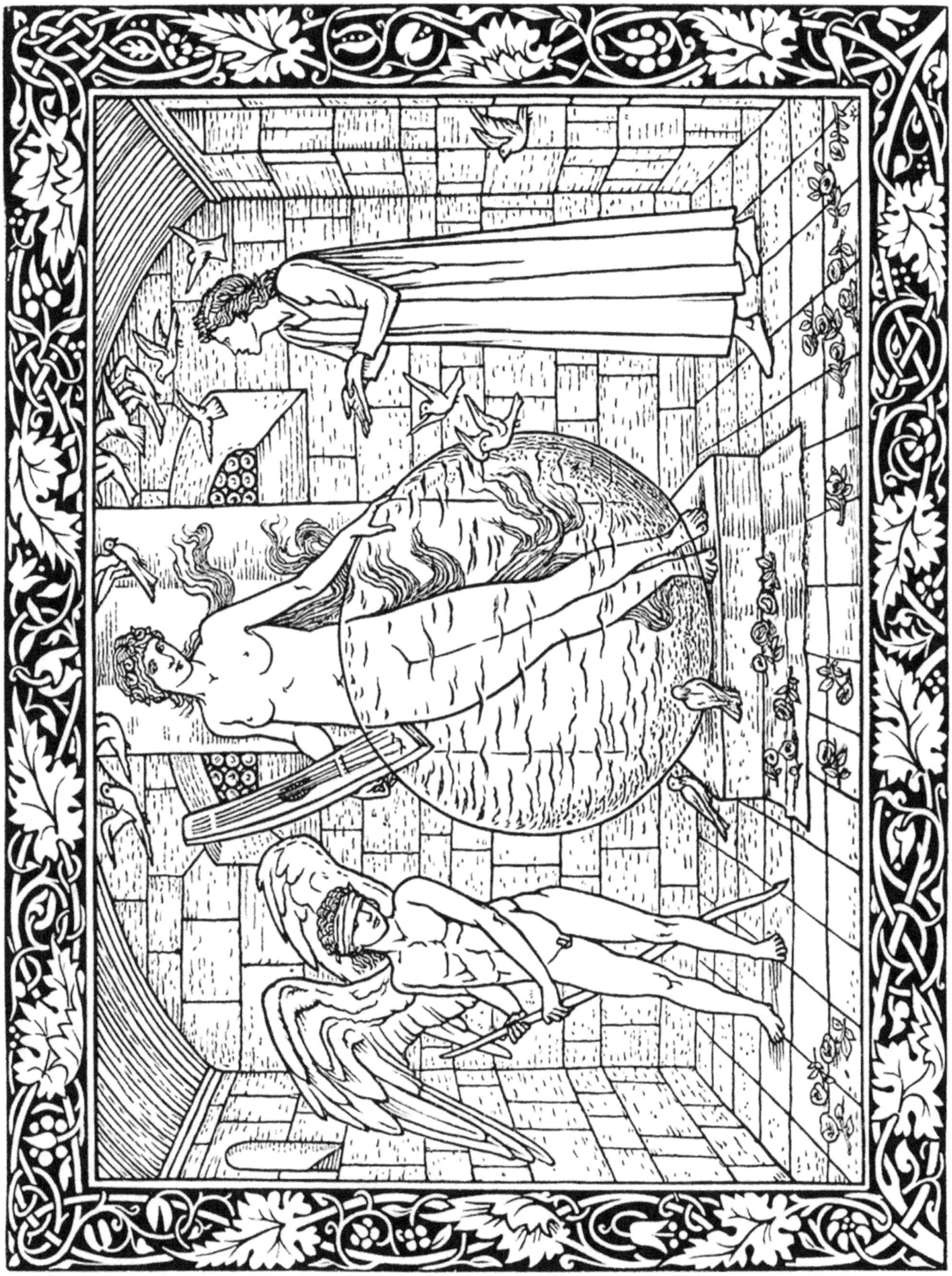

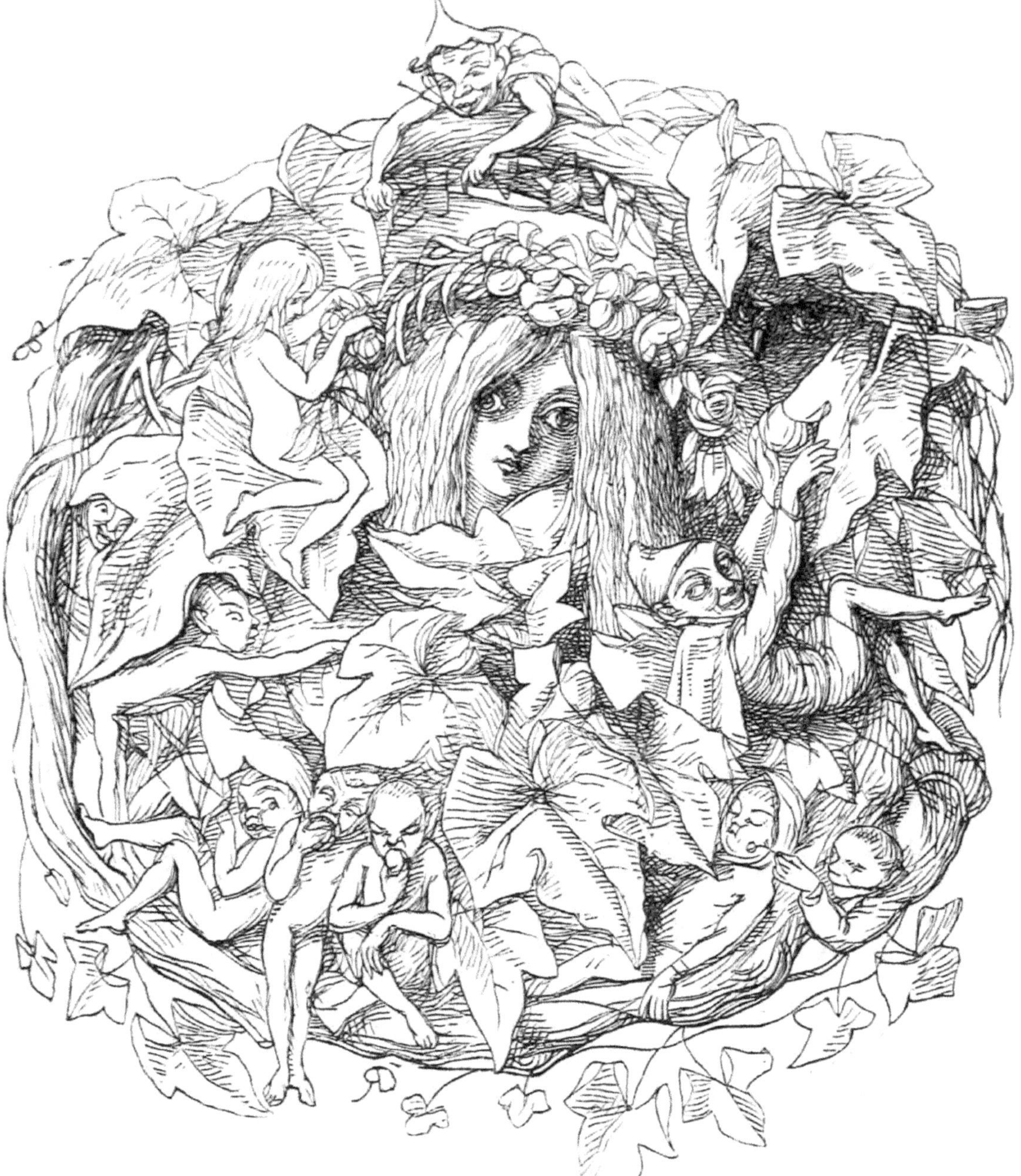

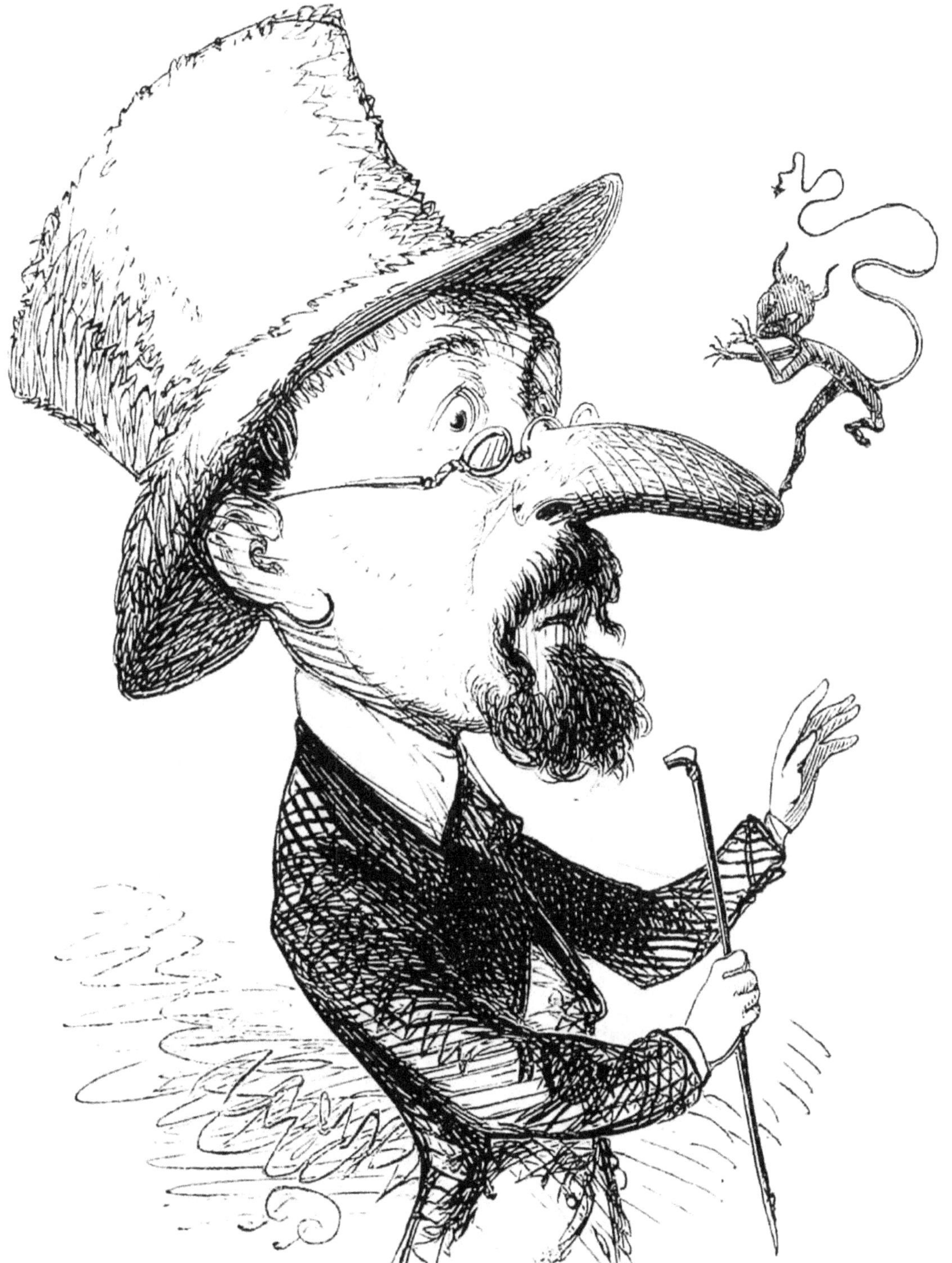

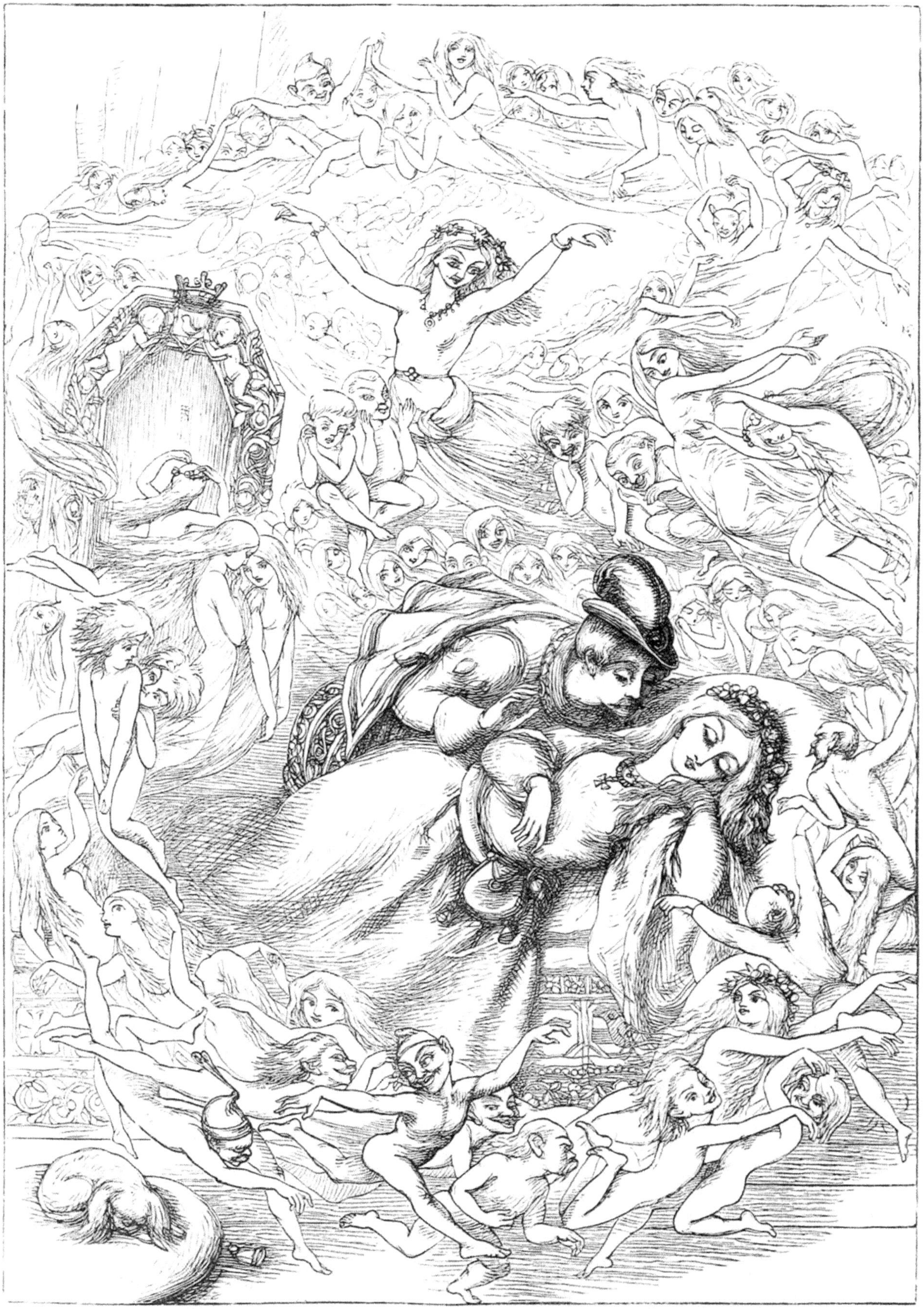

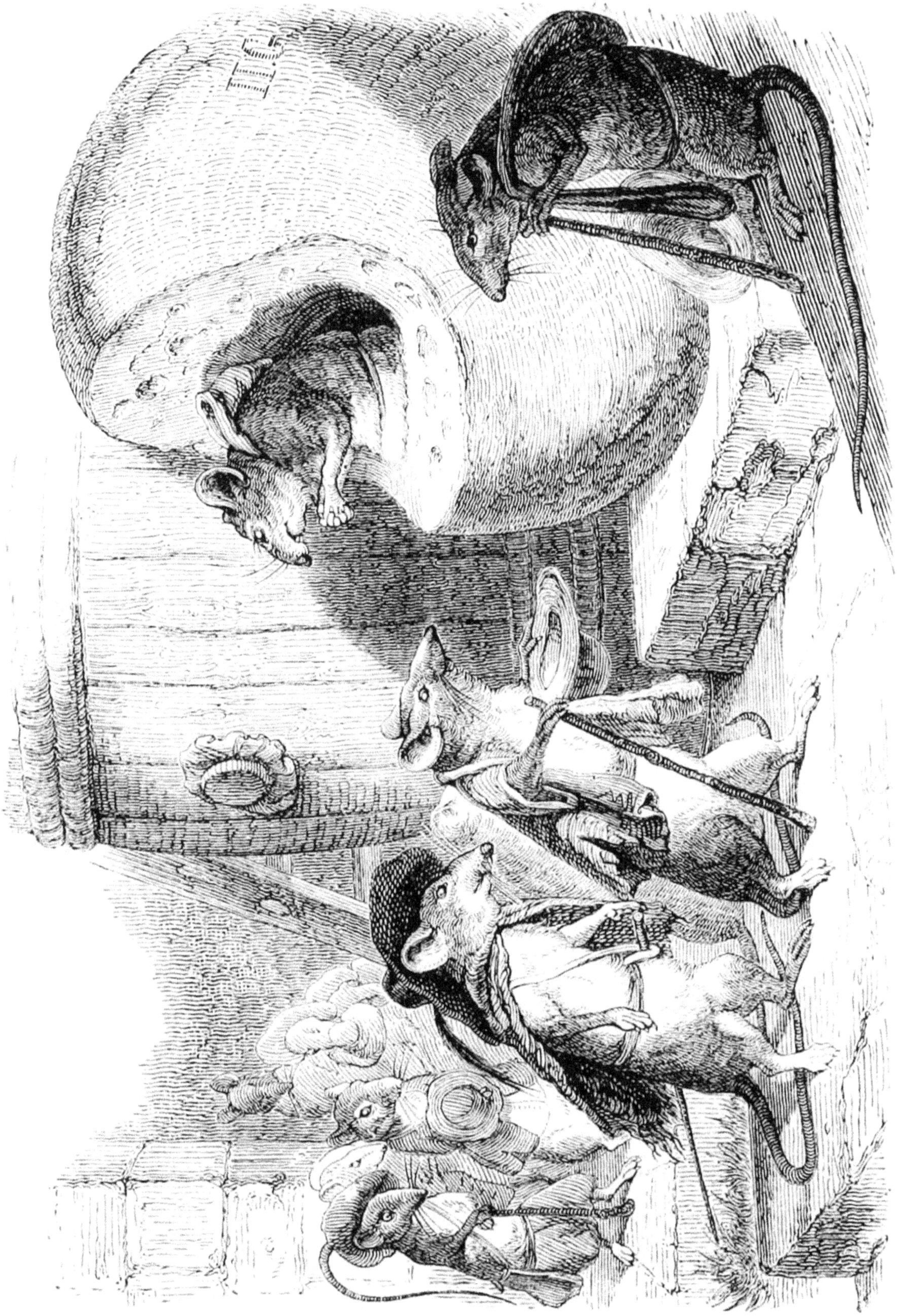

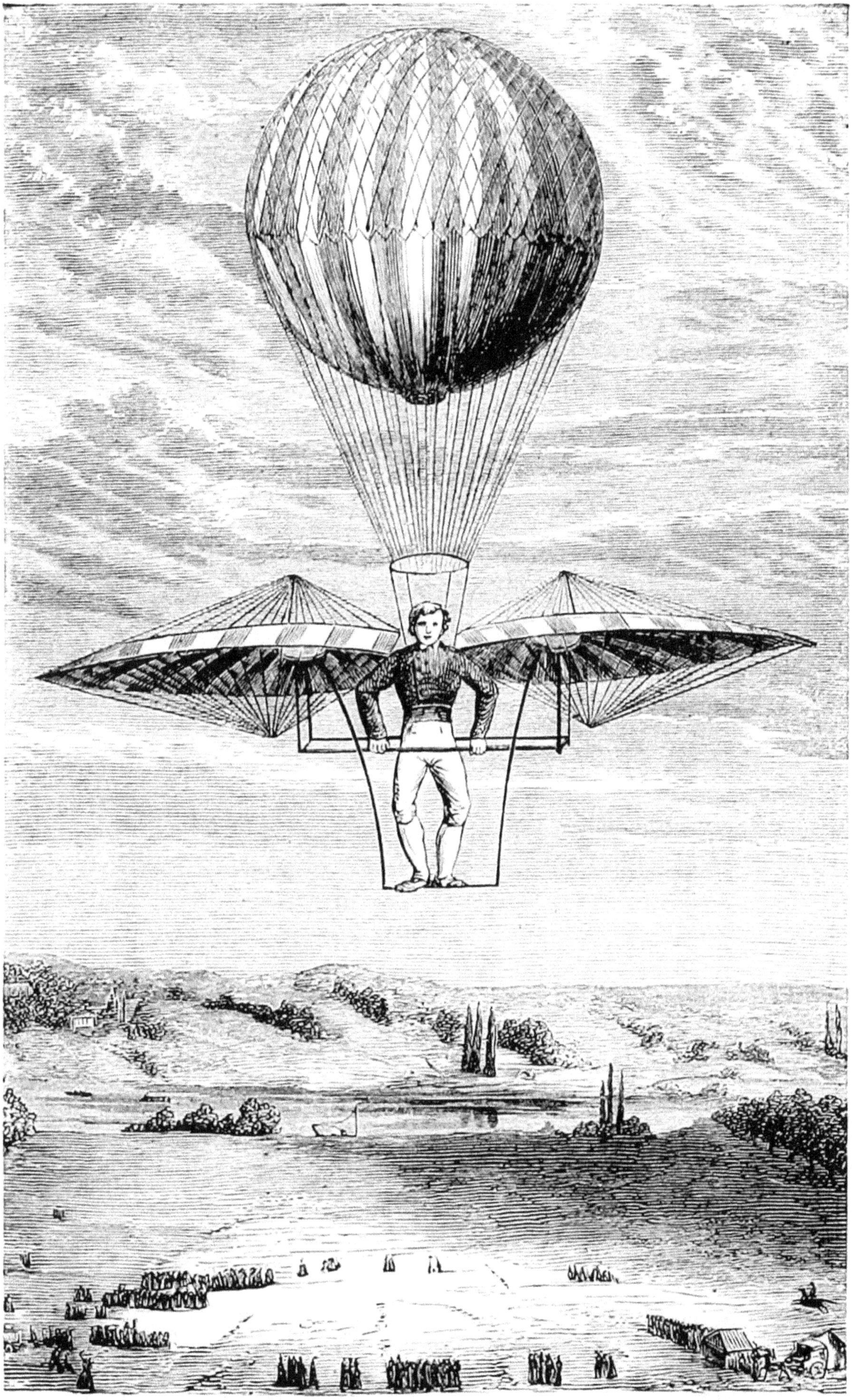

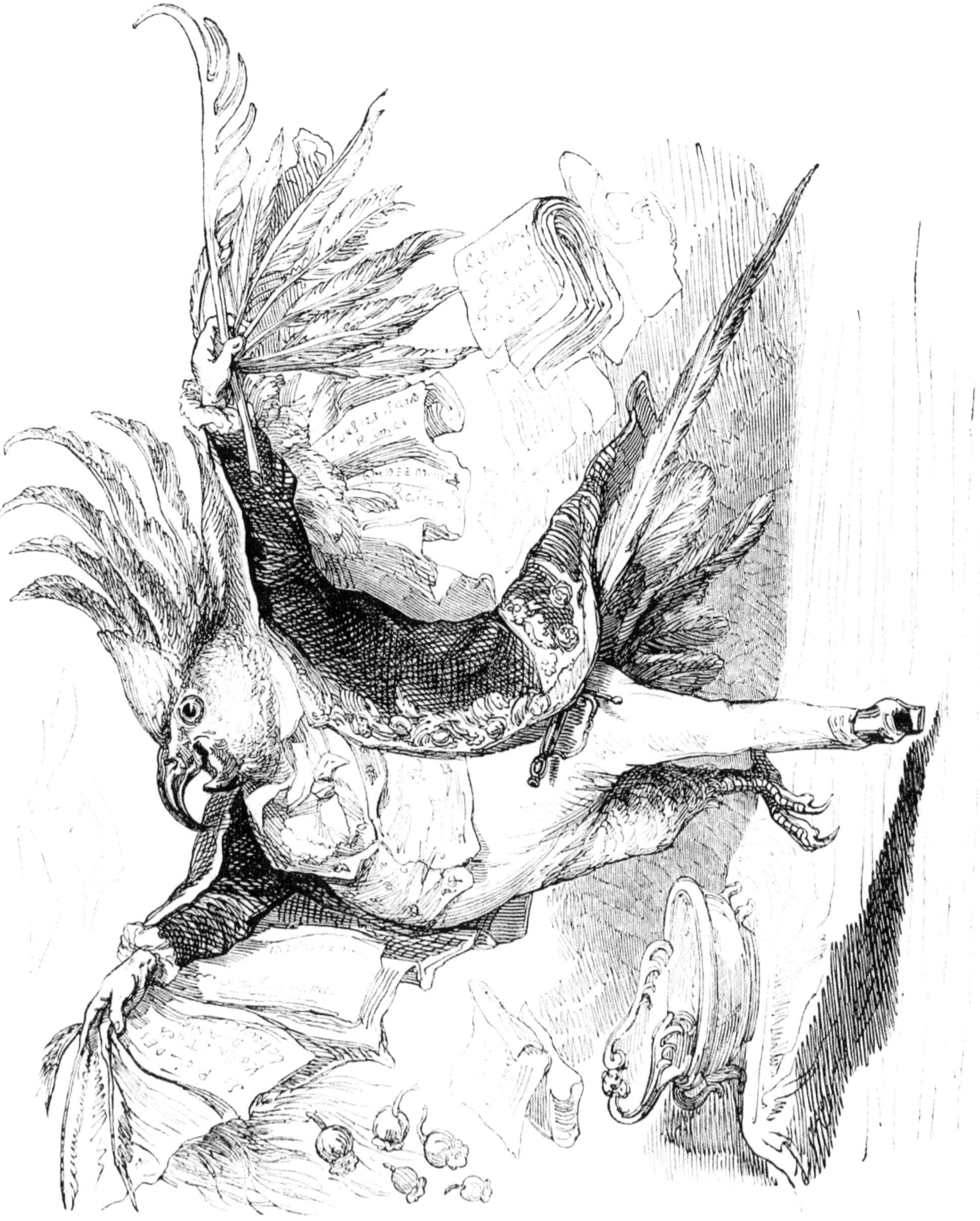

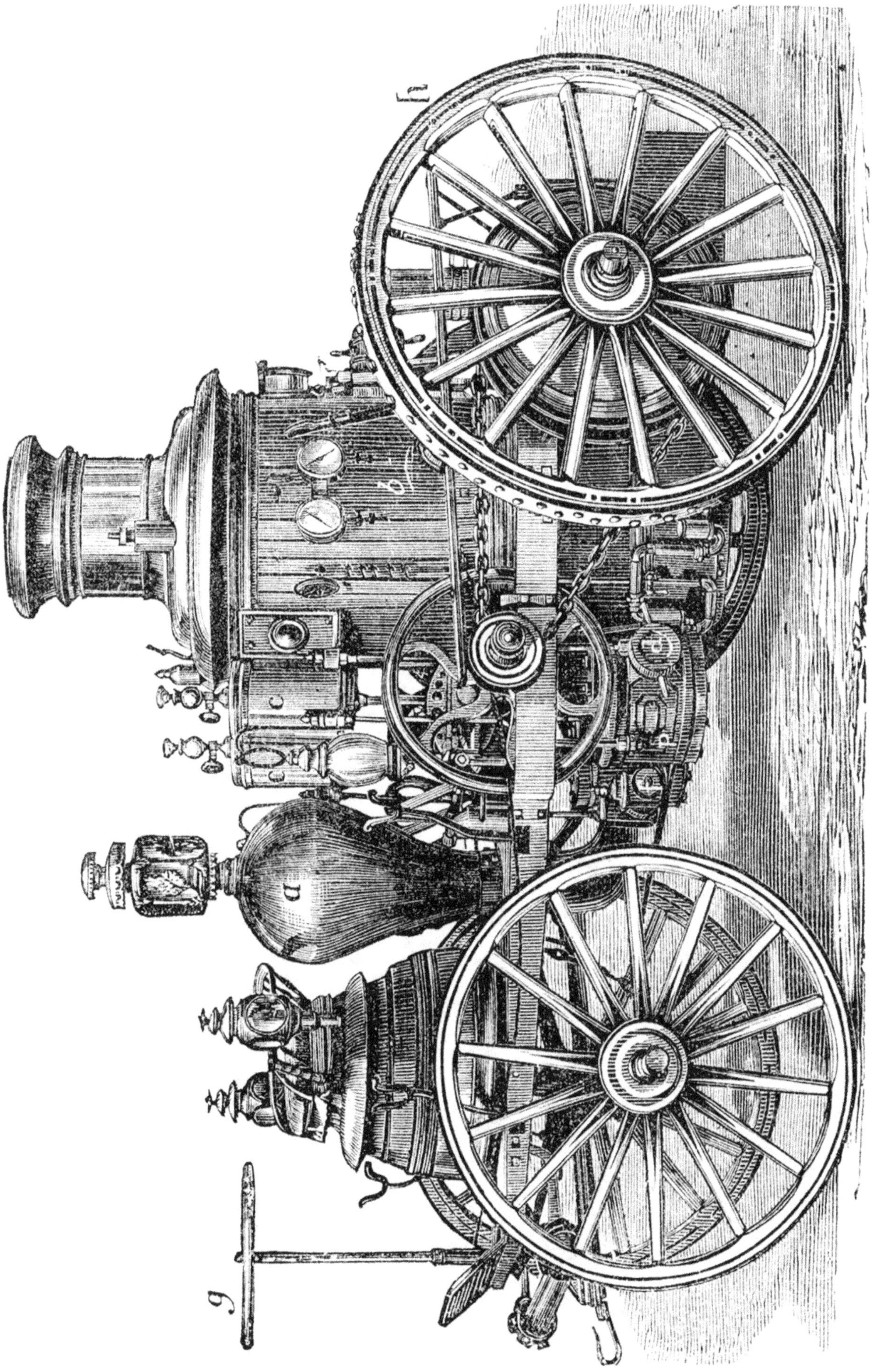

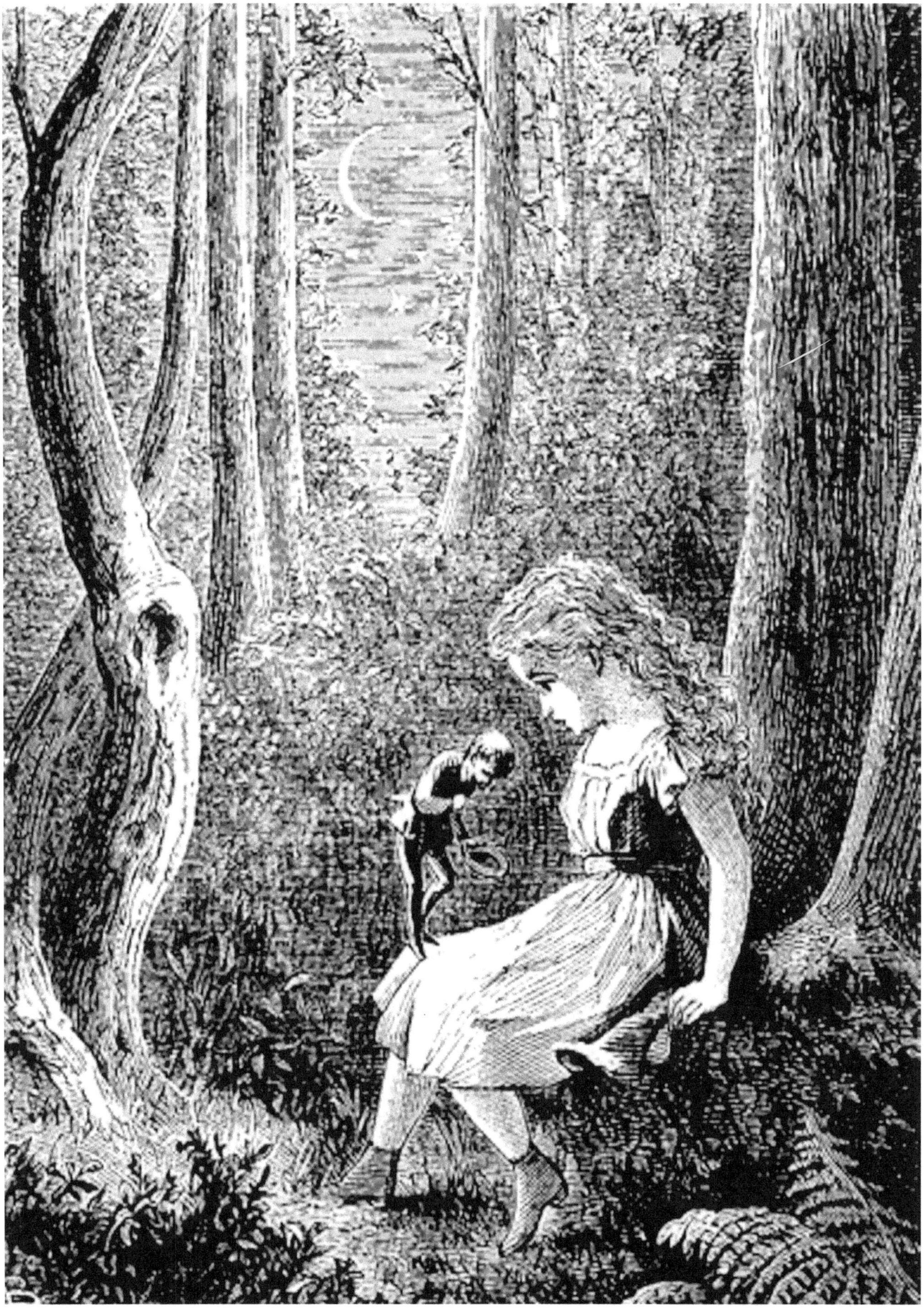

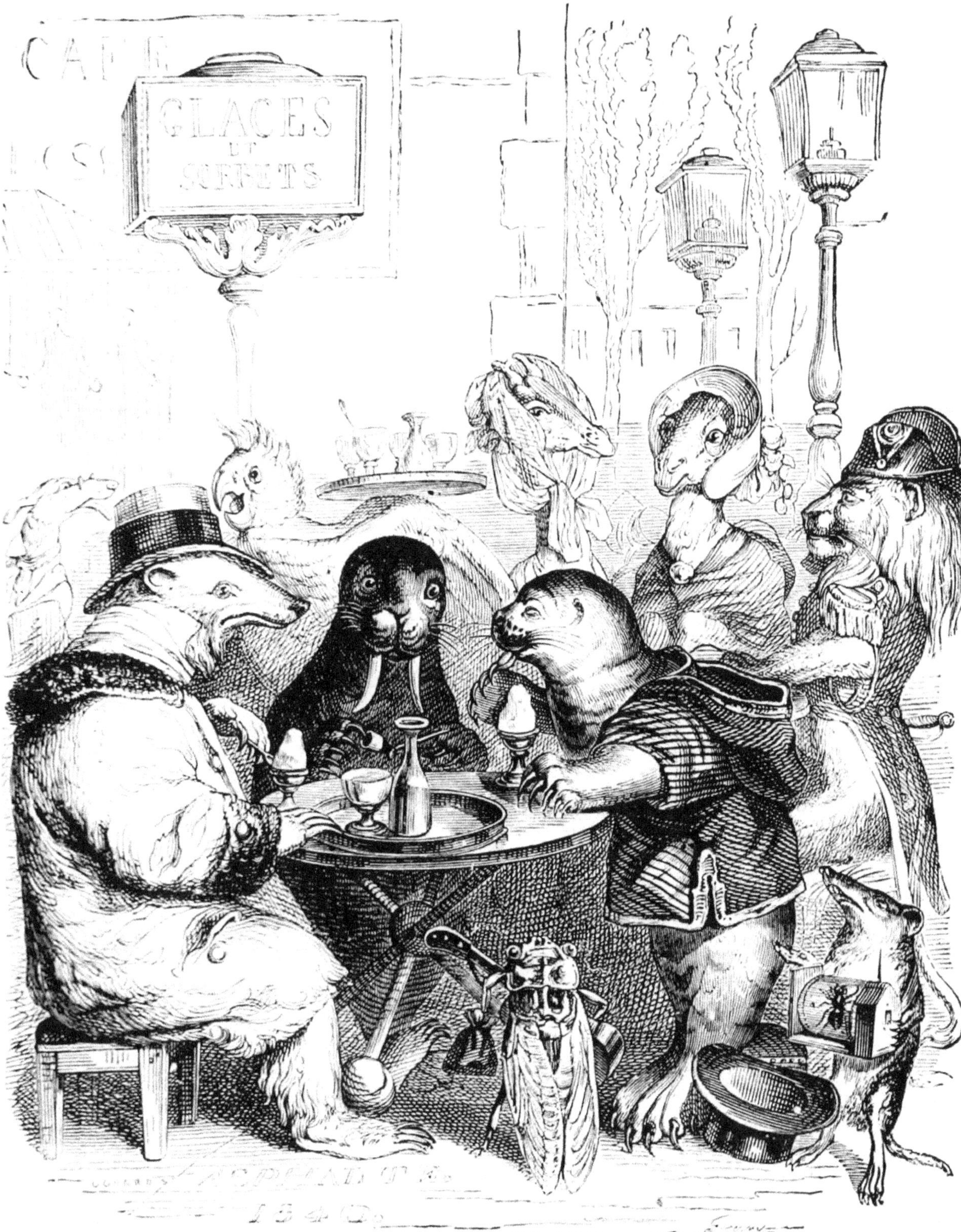
GLACES
SORBETS
1840

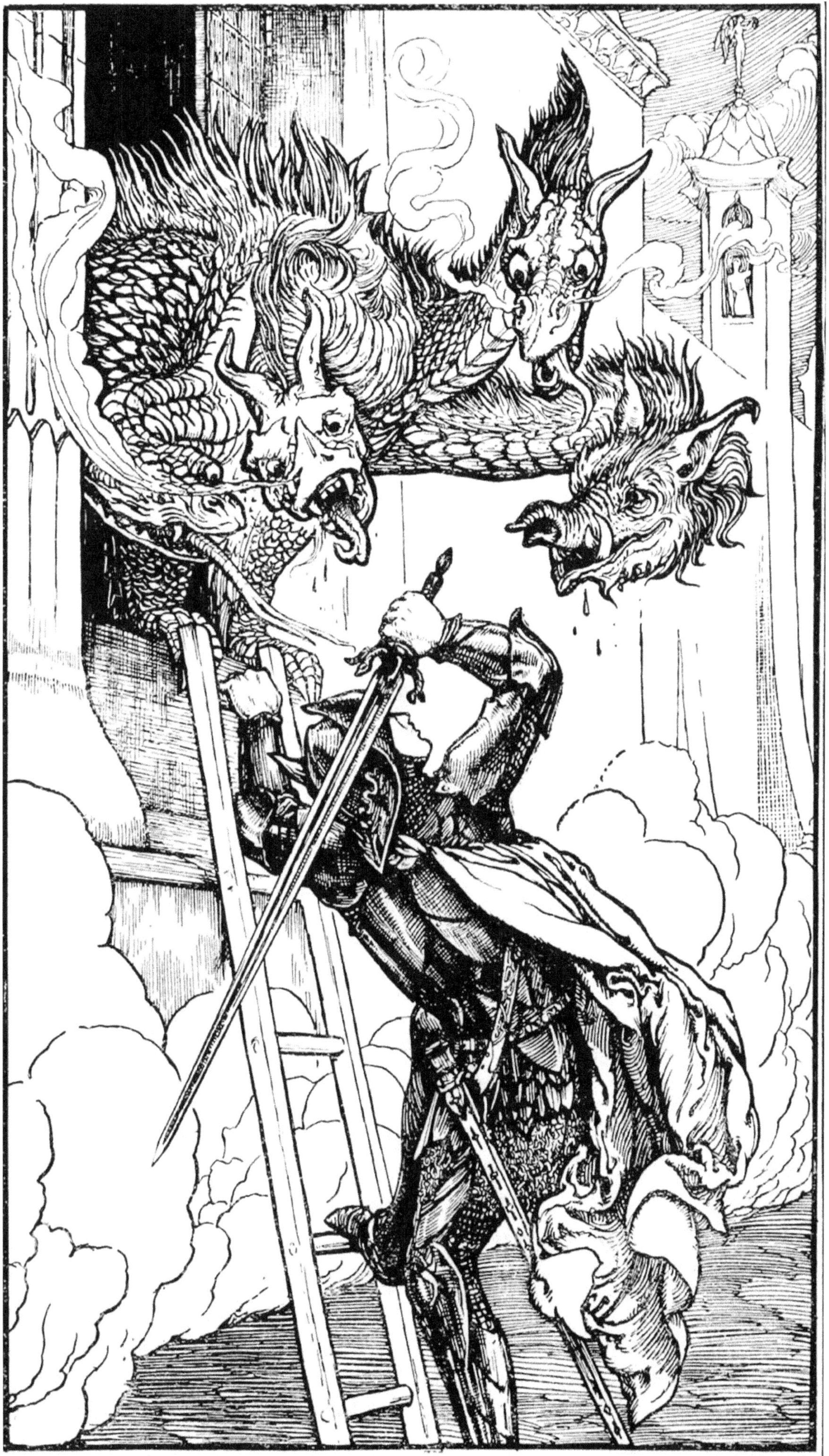

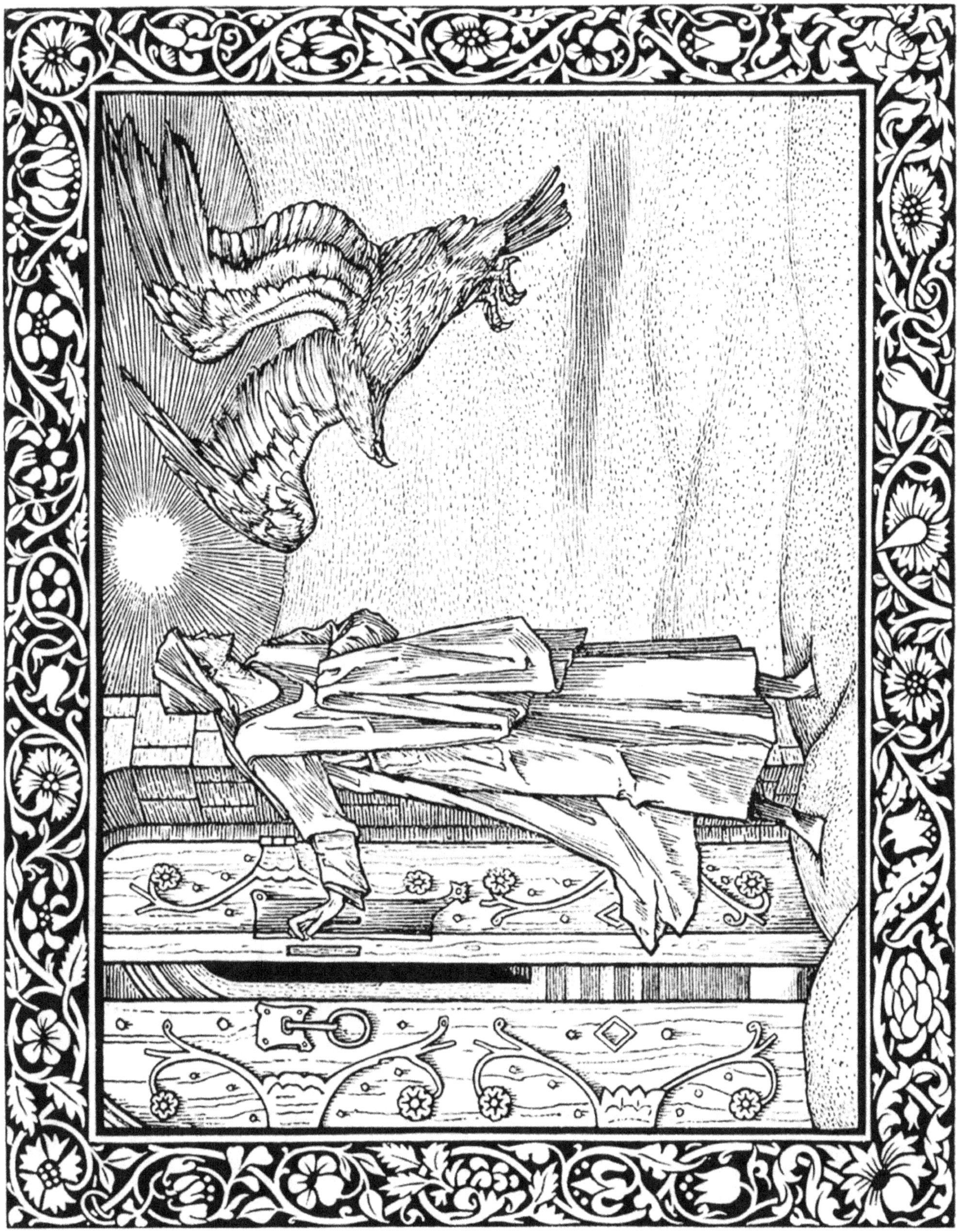

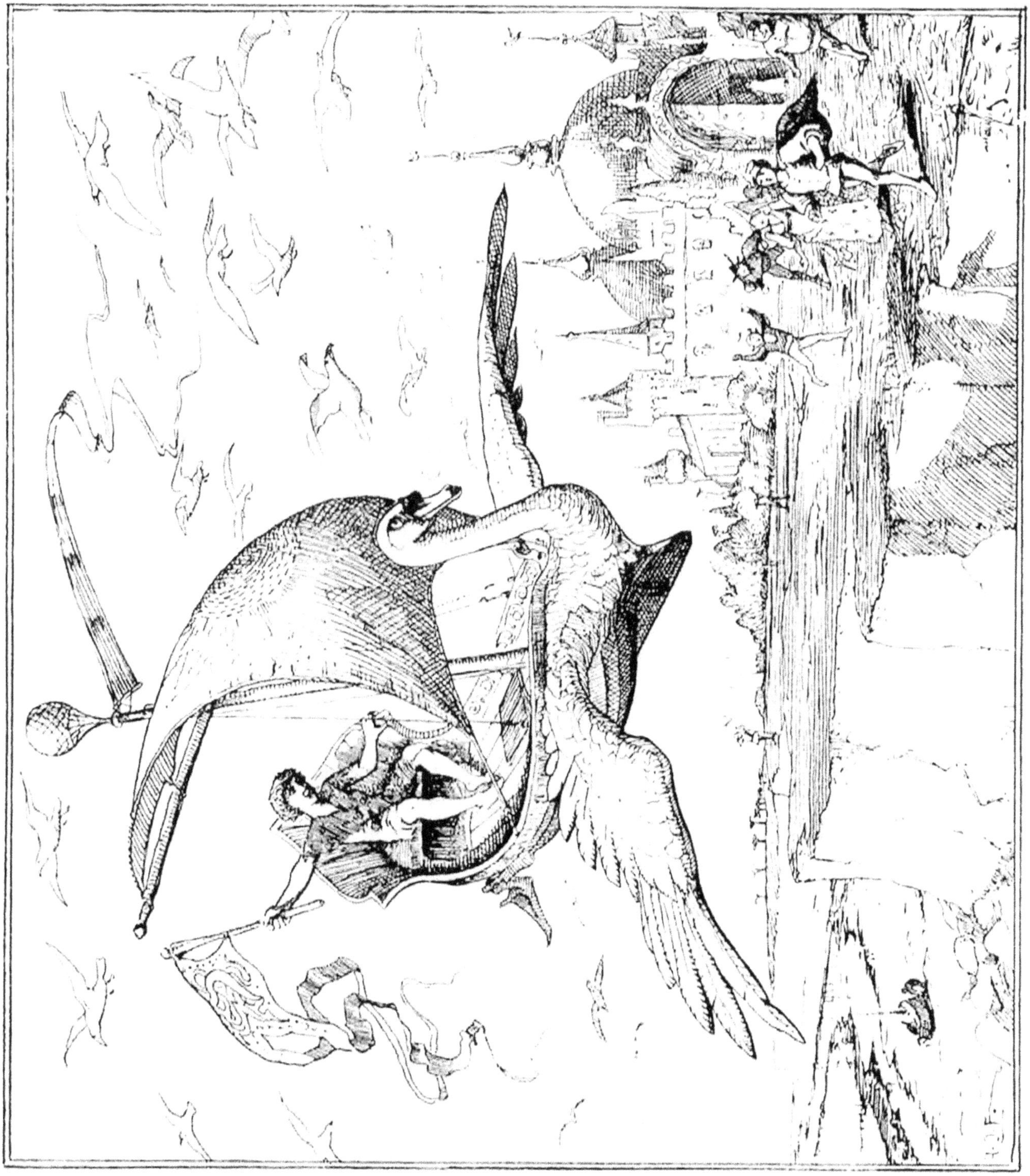

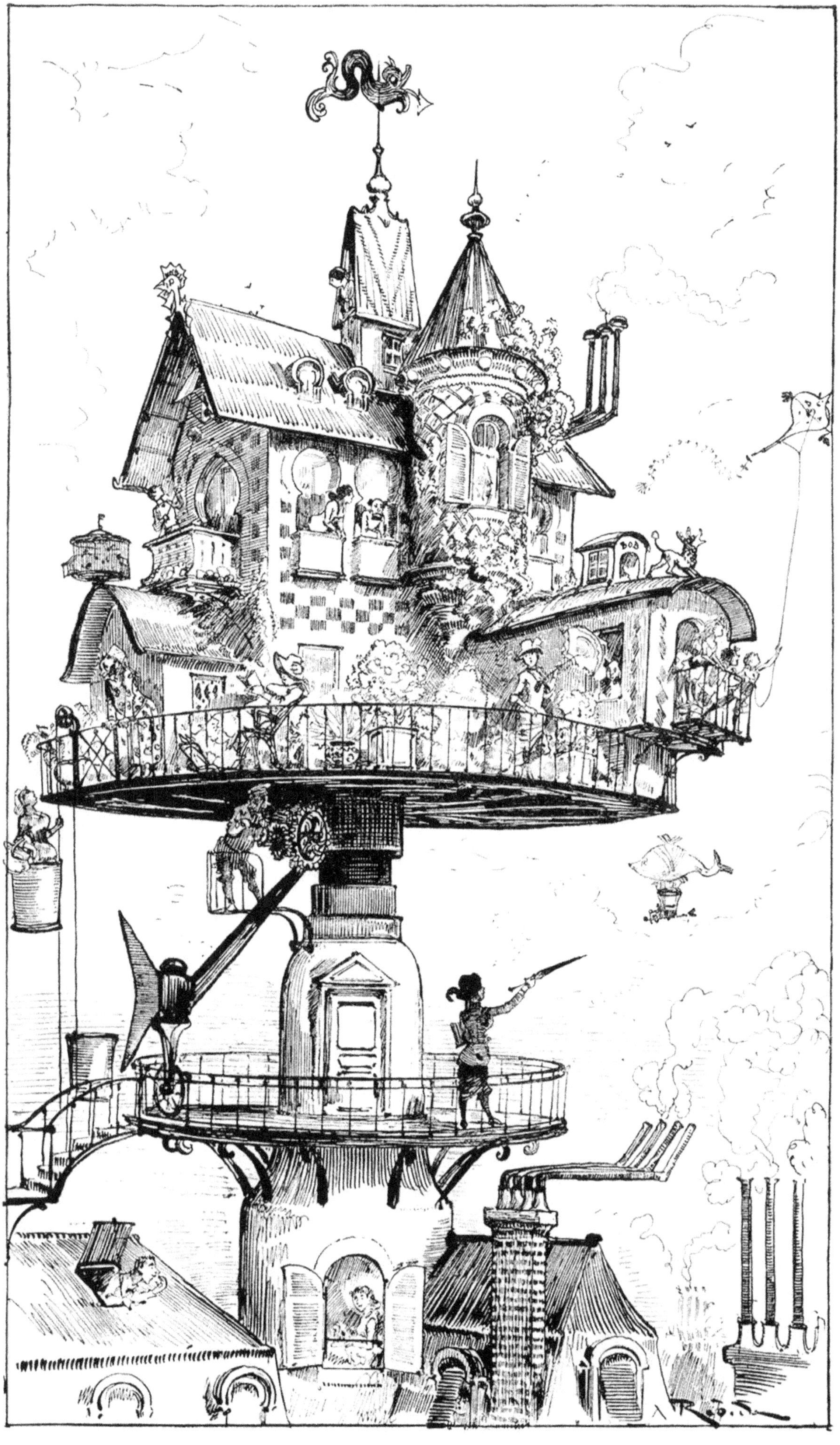

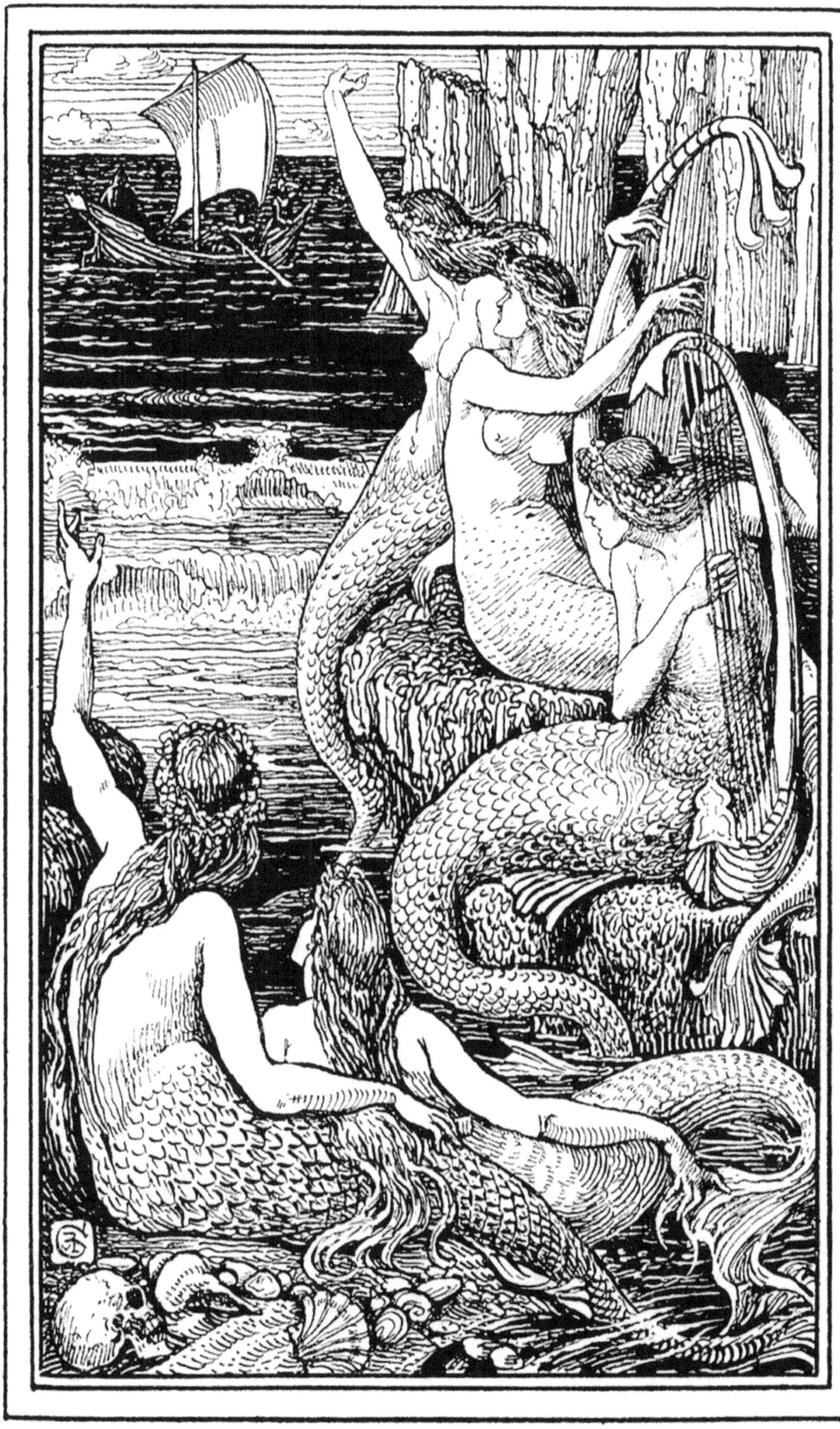

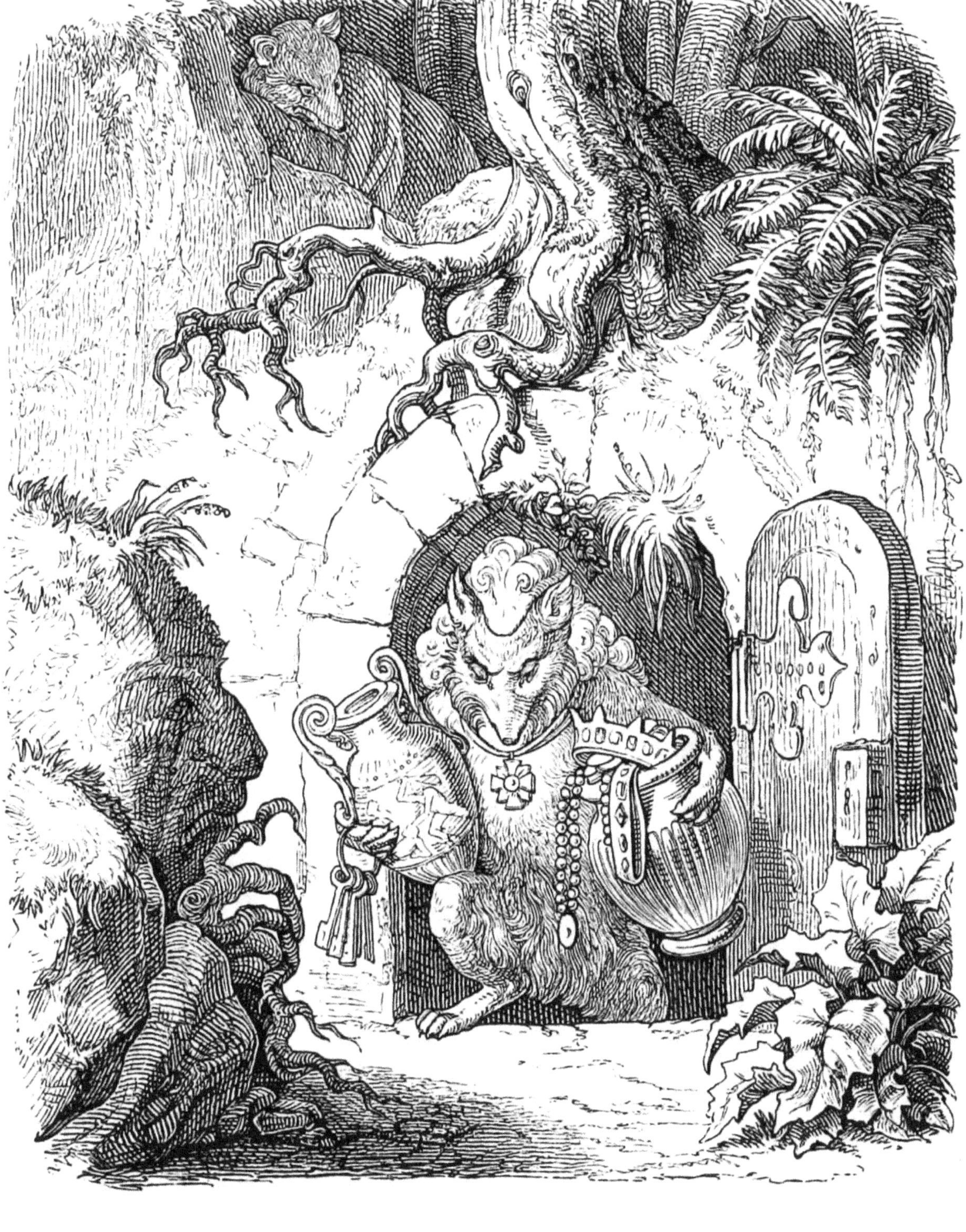

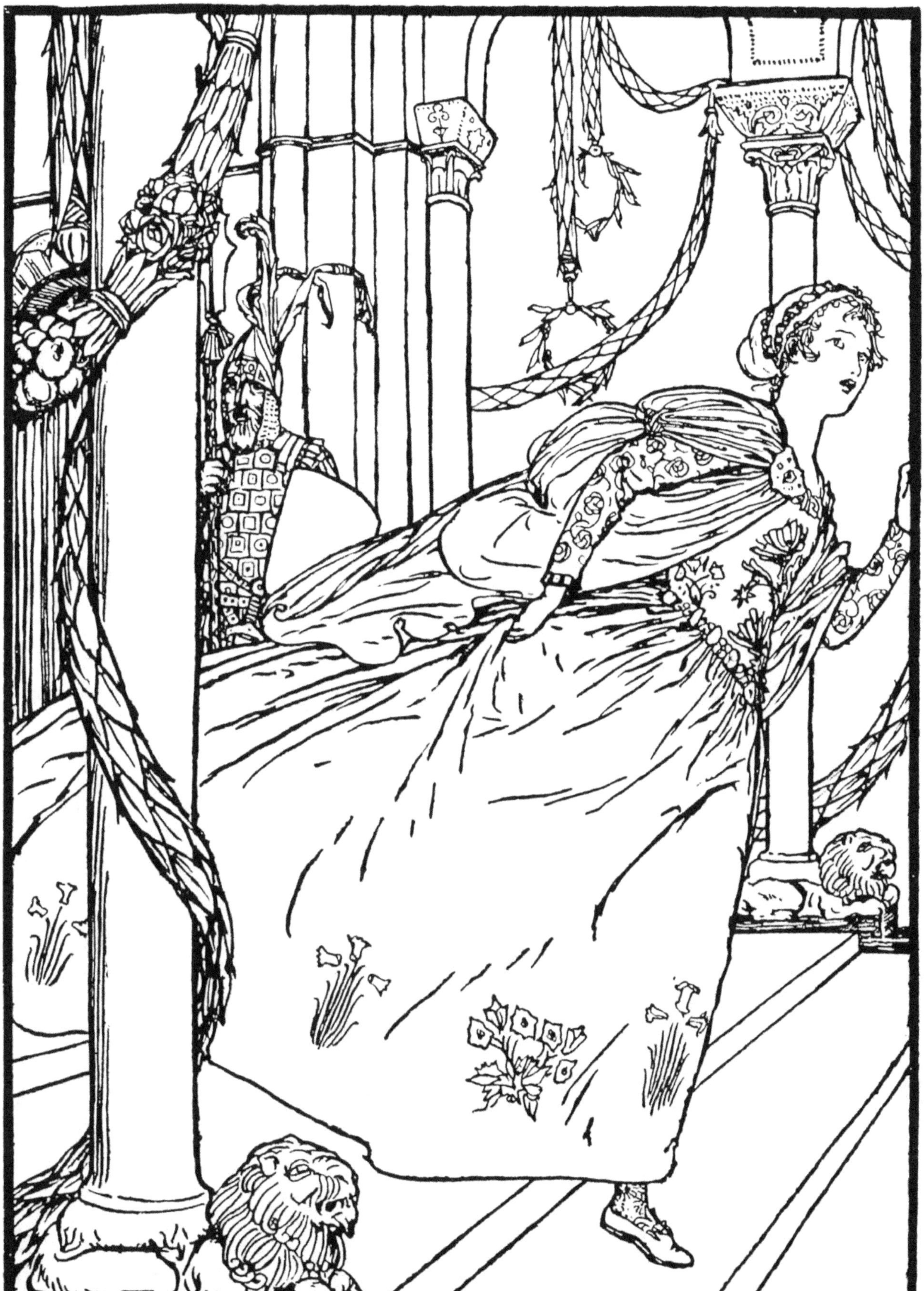

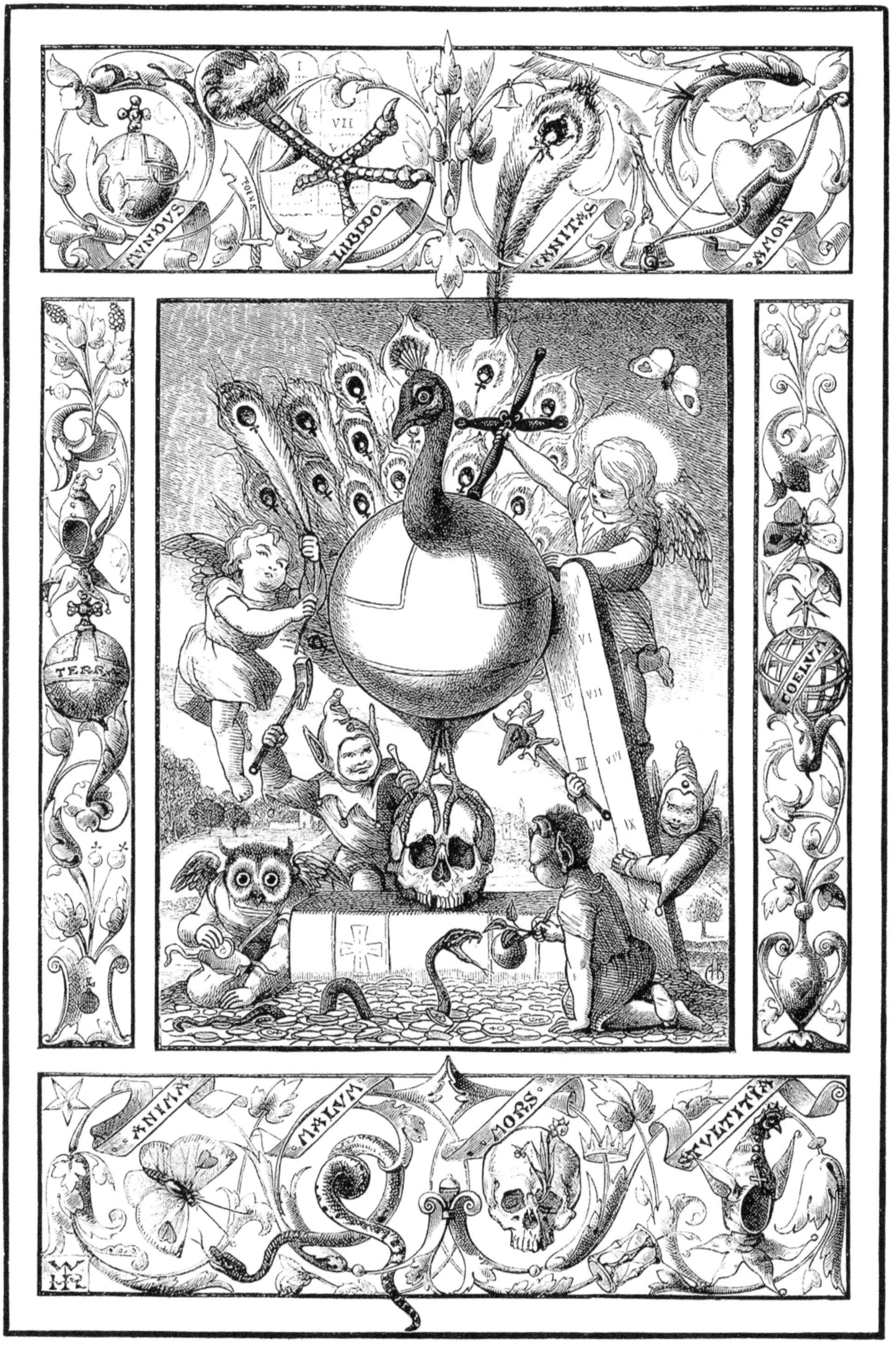
MVNDVS
LIBIDO
VANITAS
AMOR
COELVM
ANIMA
MALVM
MORS
STVLTITIA

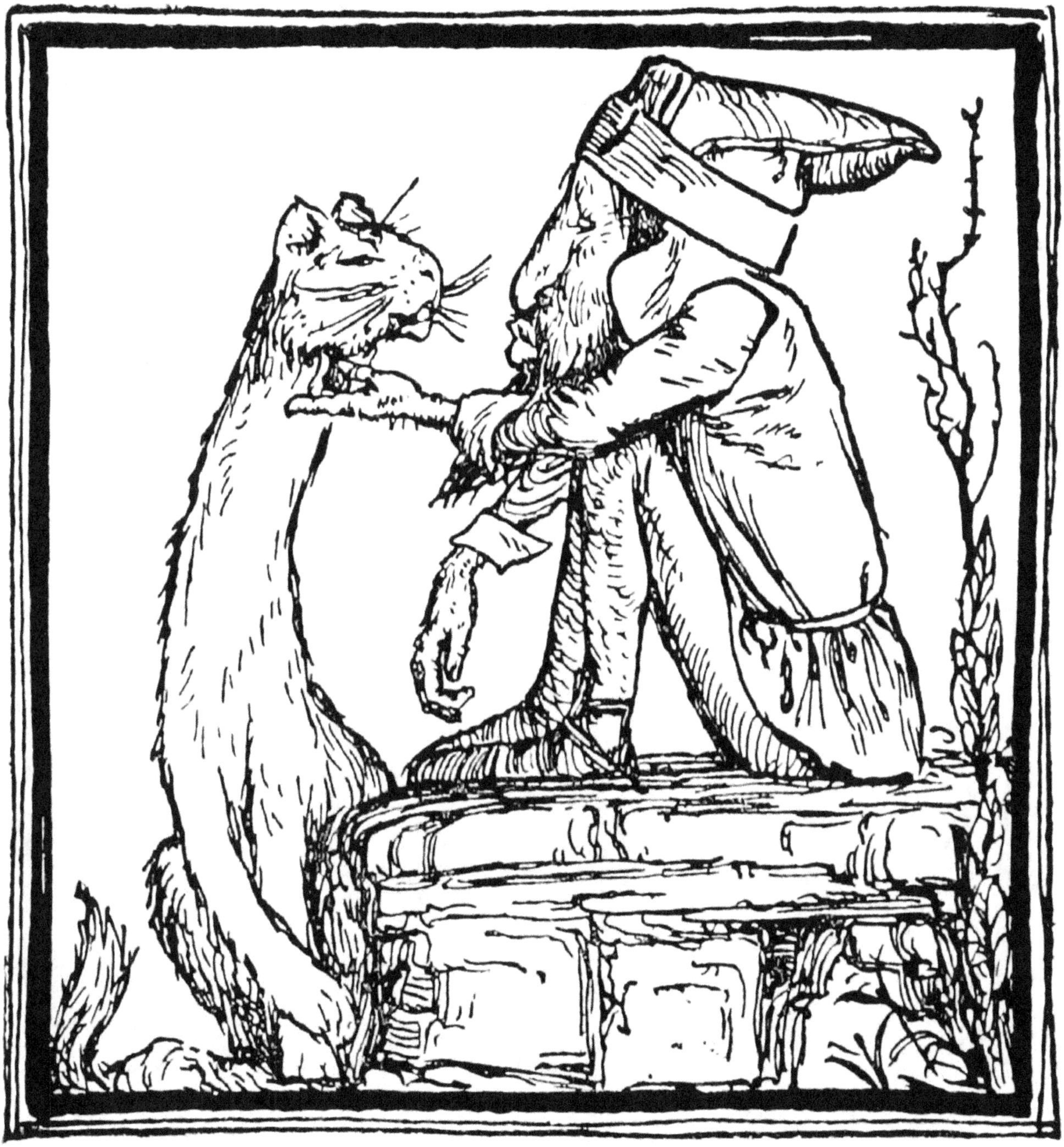

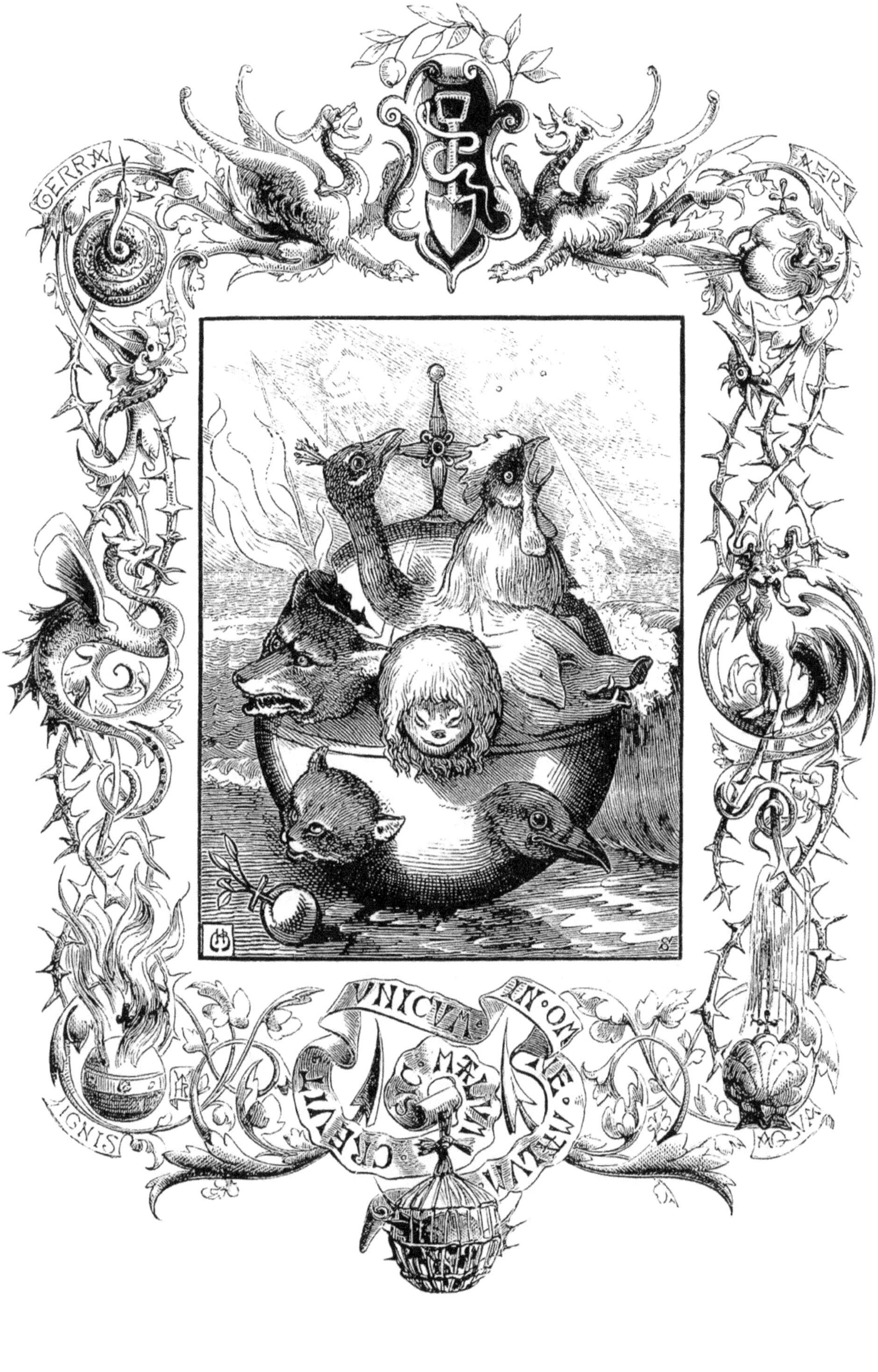

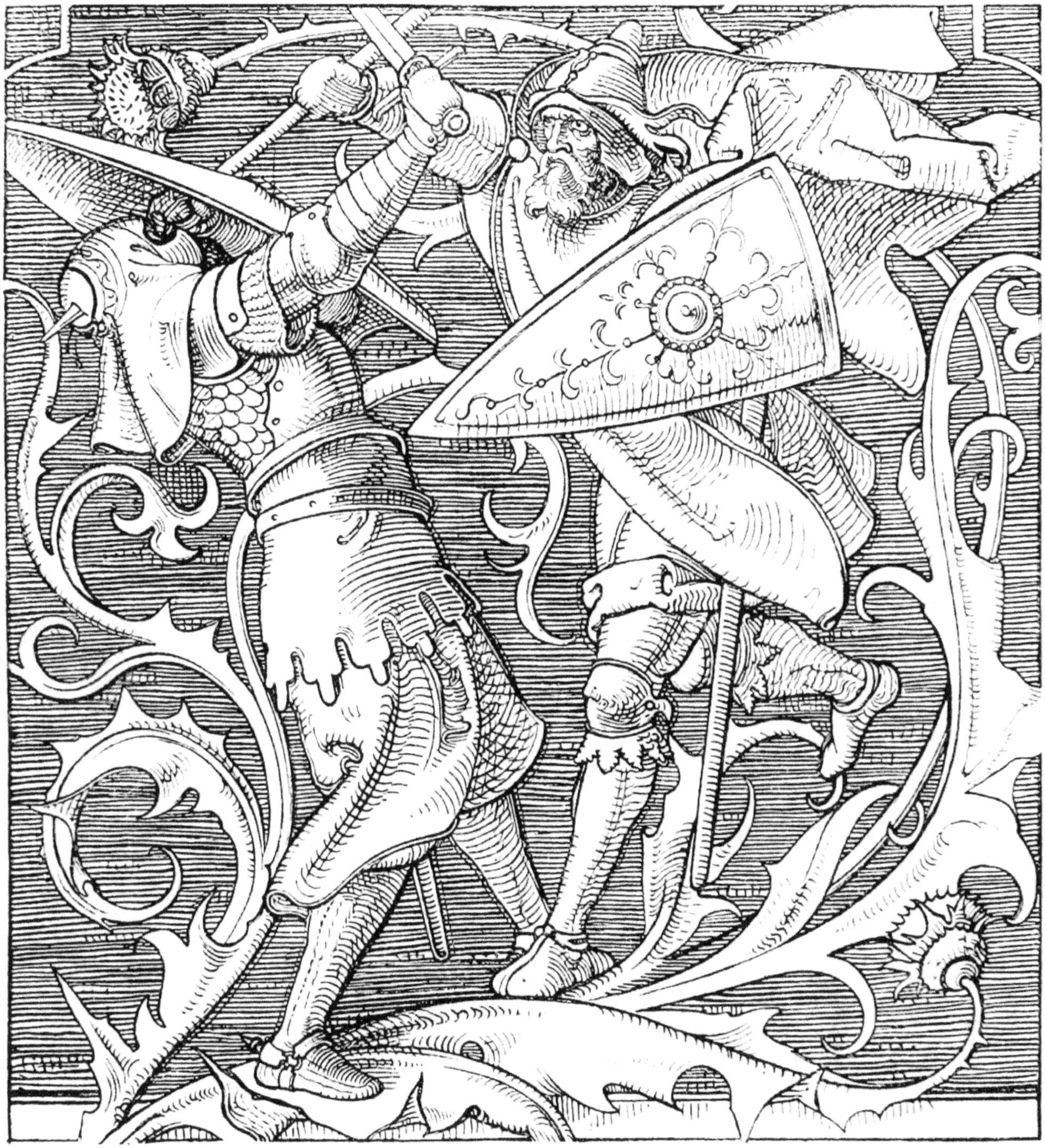

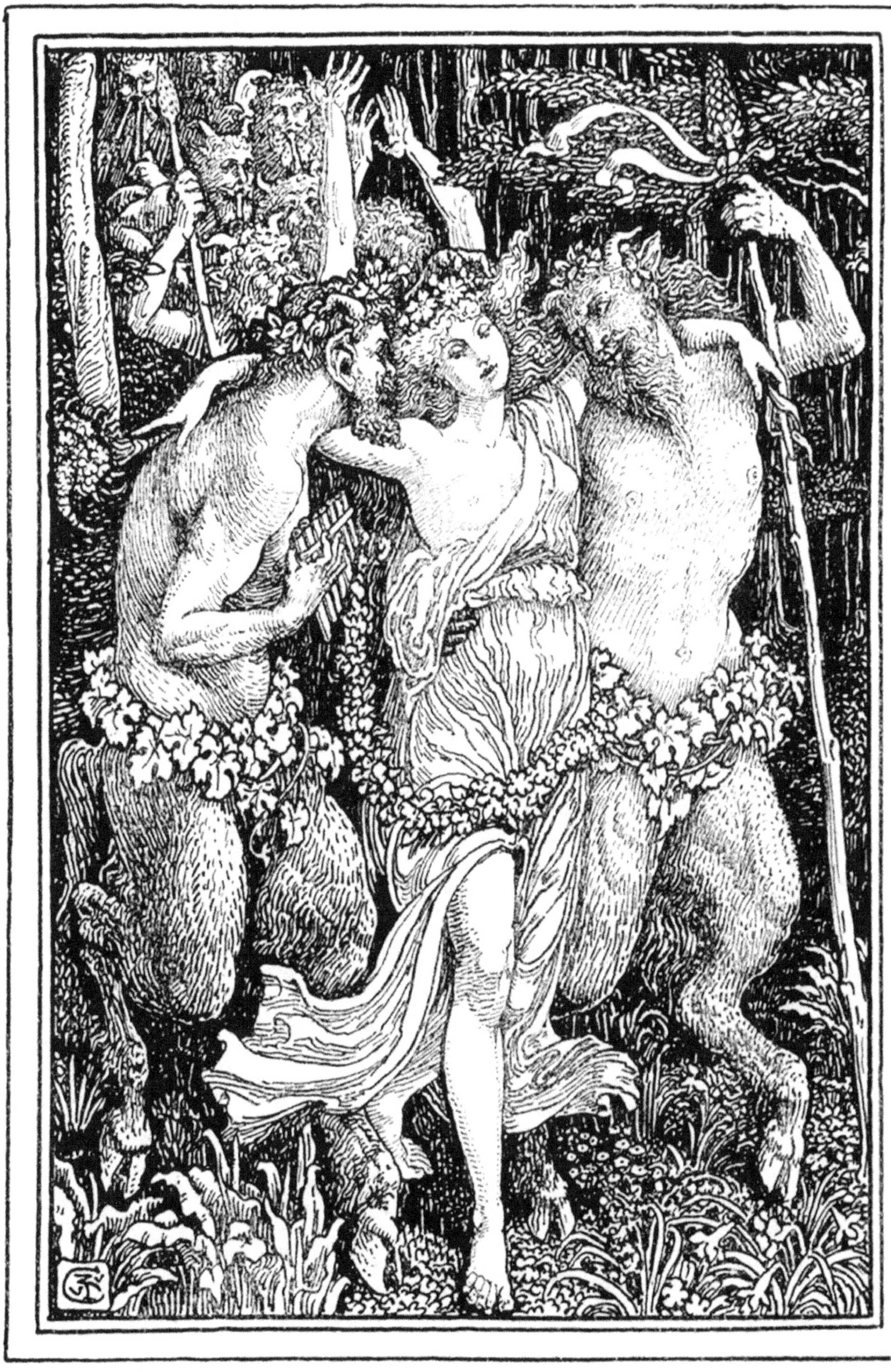

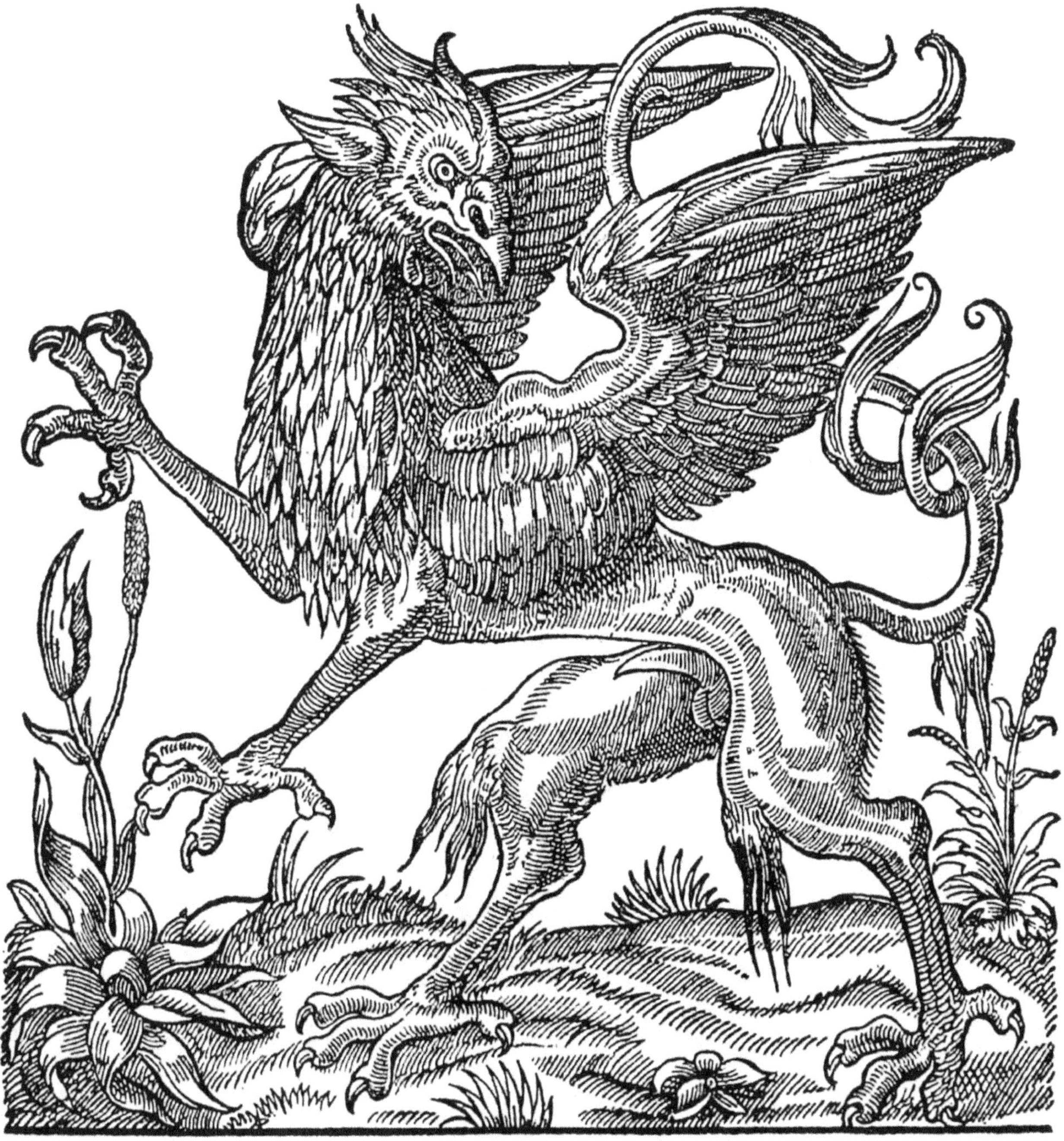

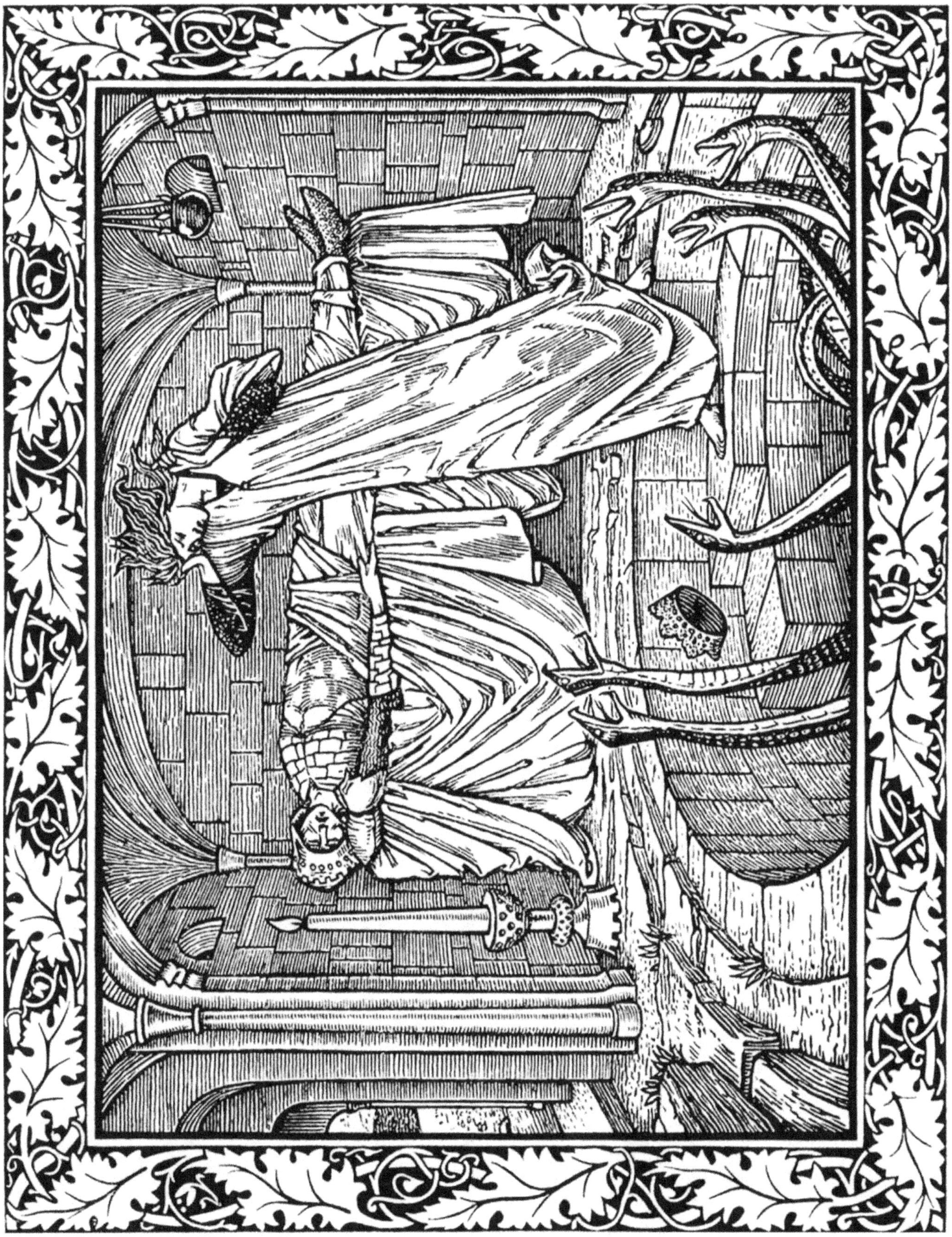

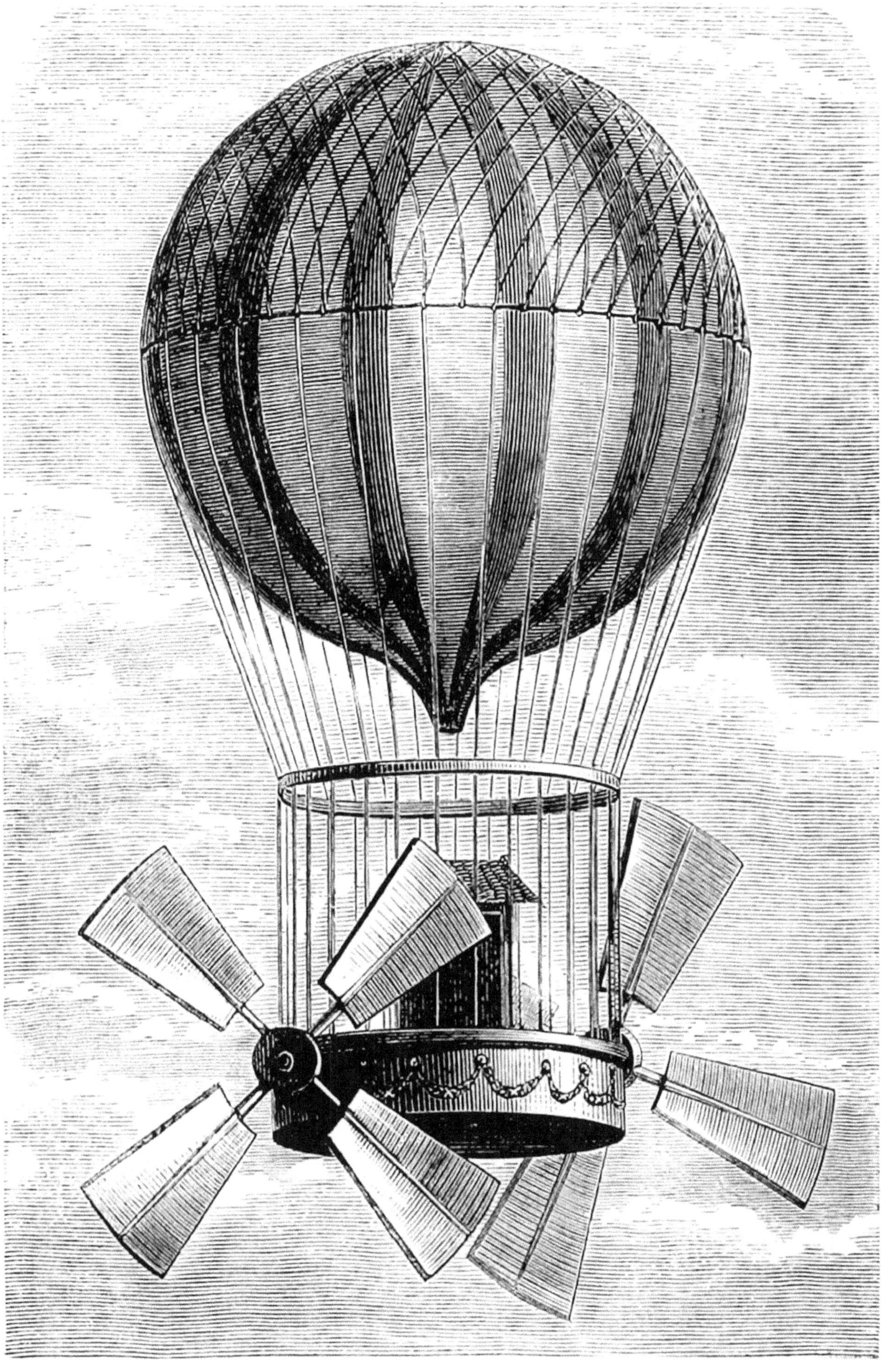

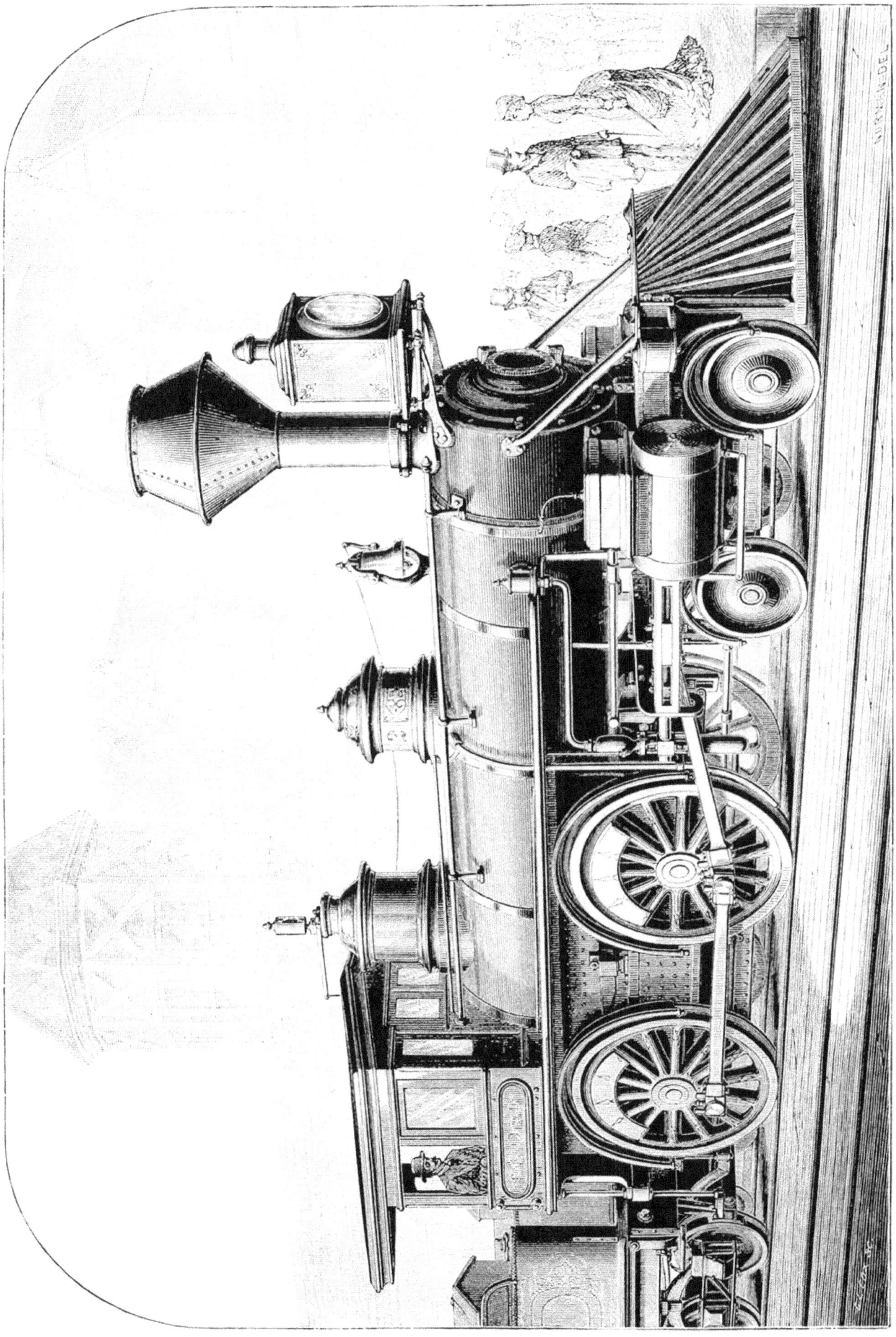

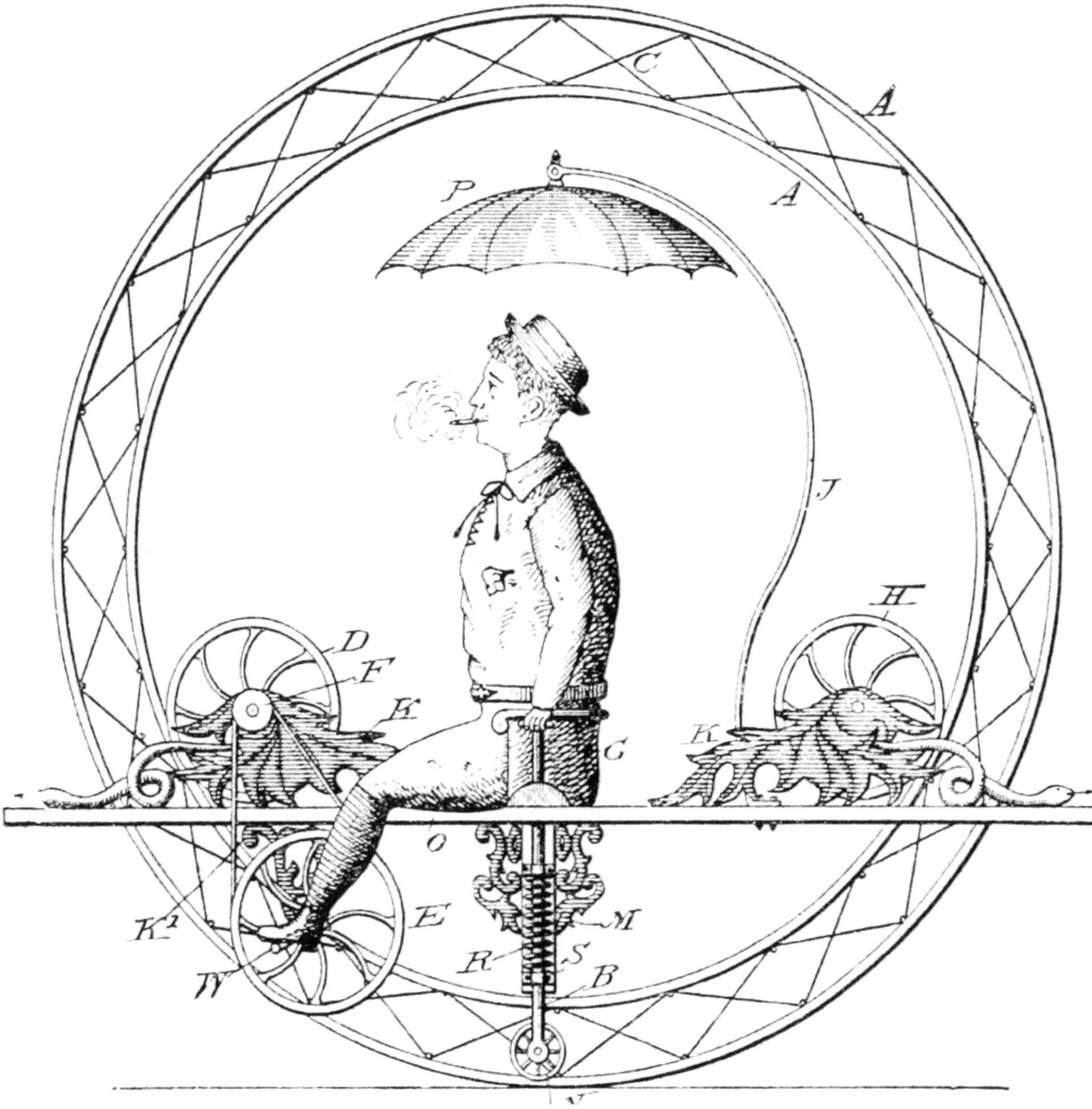

C
A
P
A
J
H
D
F
K
K
G
O
E
M
K1
R
S
W
B

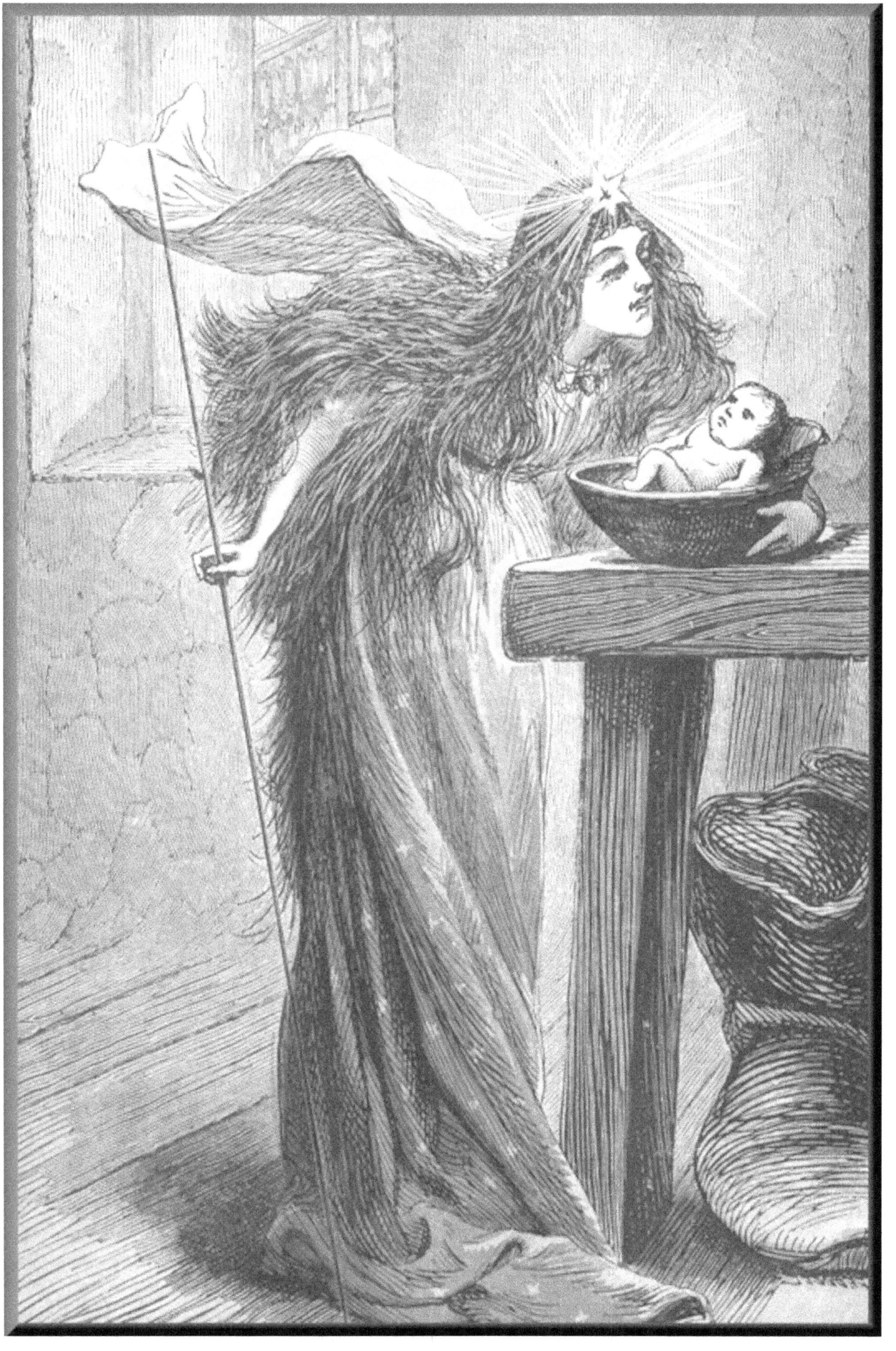

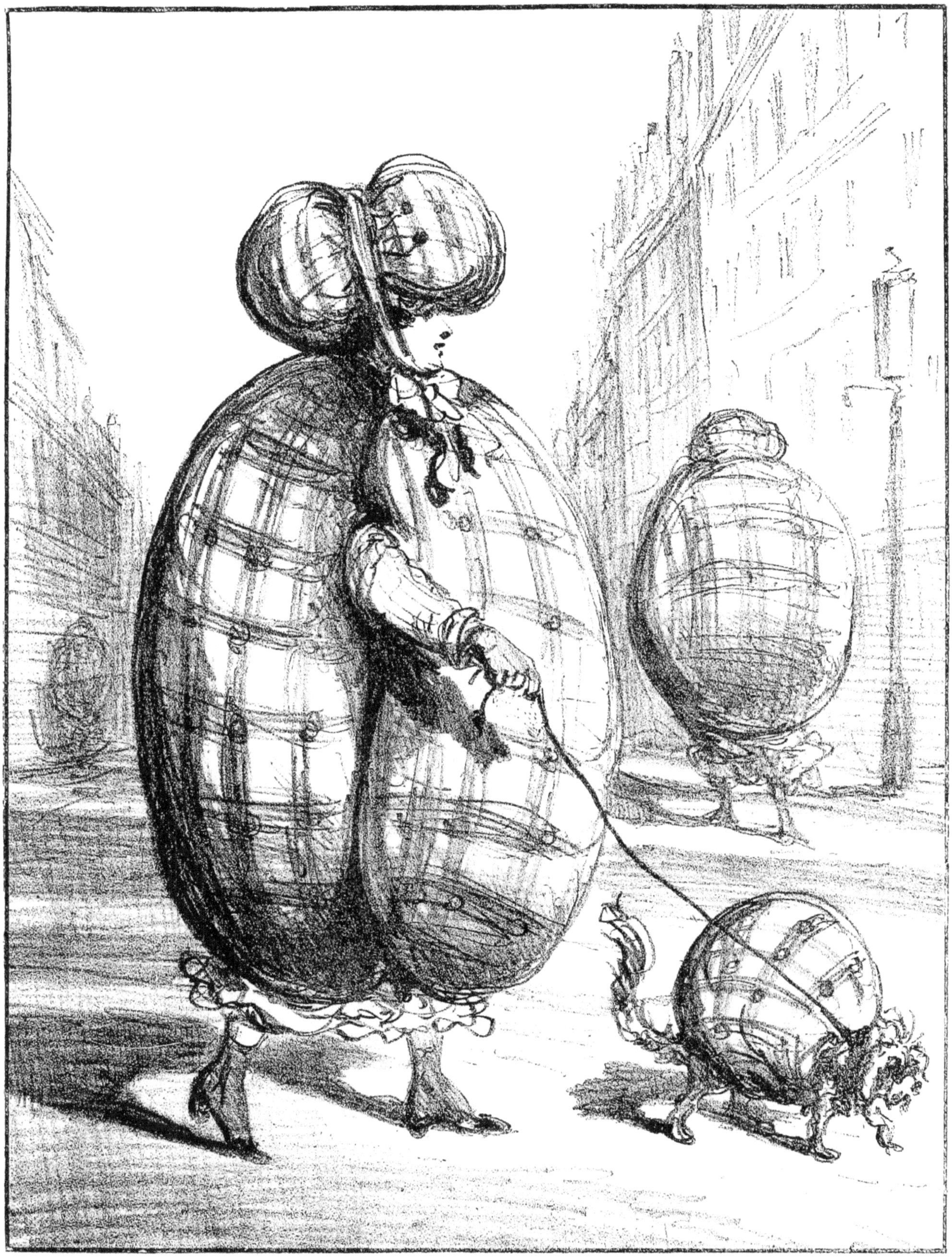

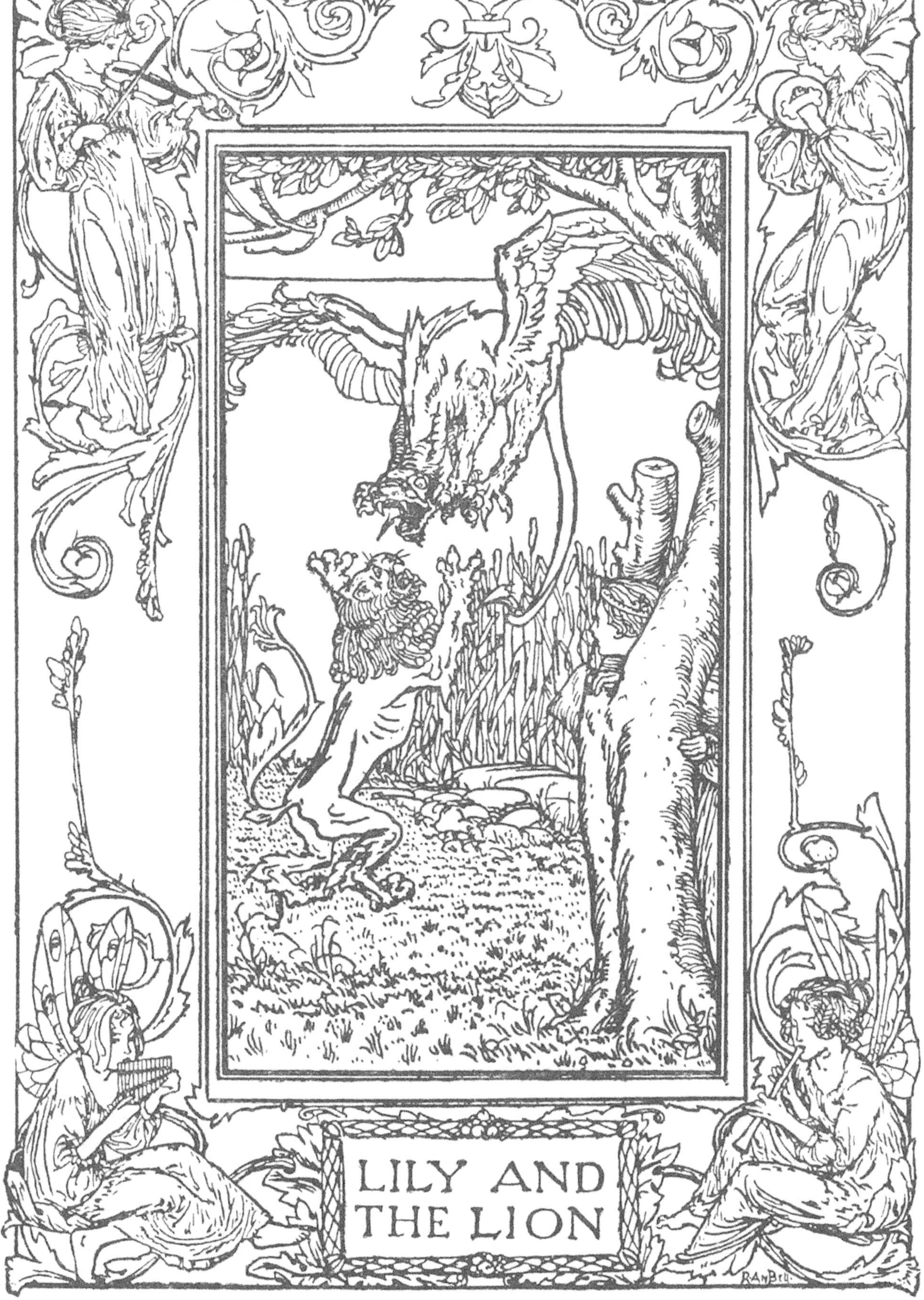
LILY AND
THE LION

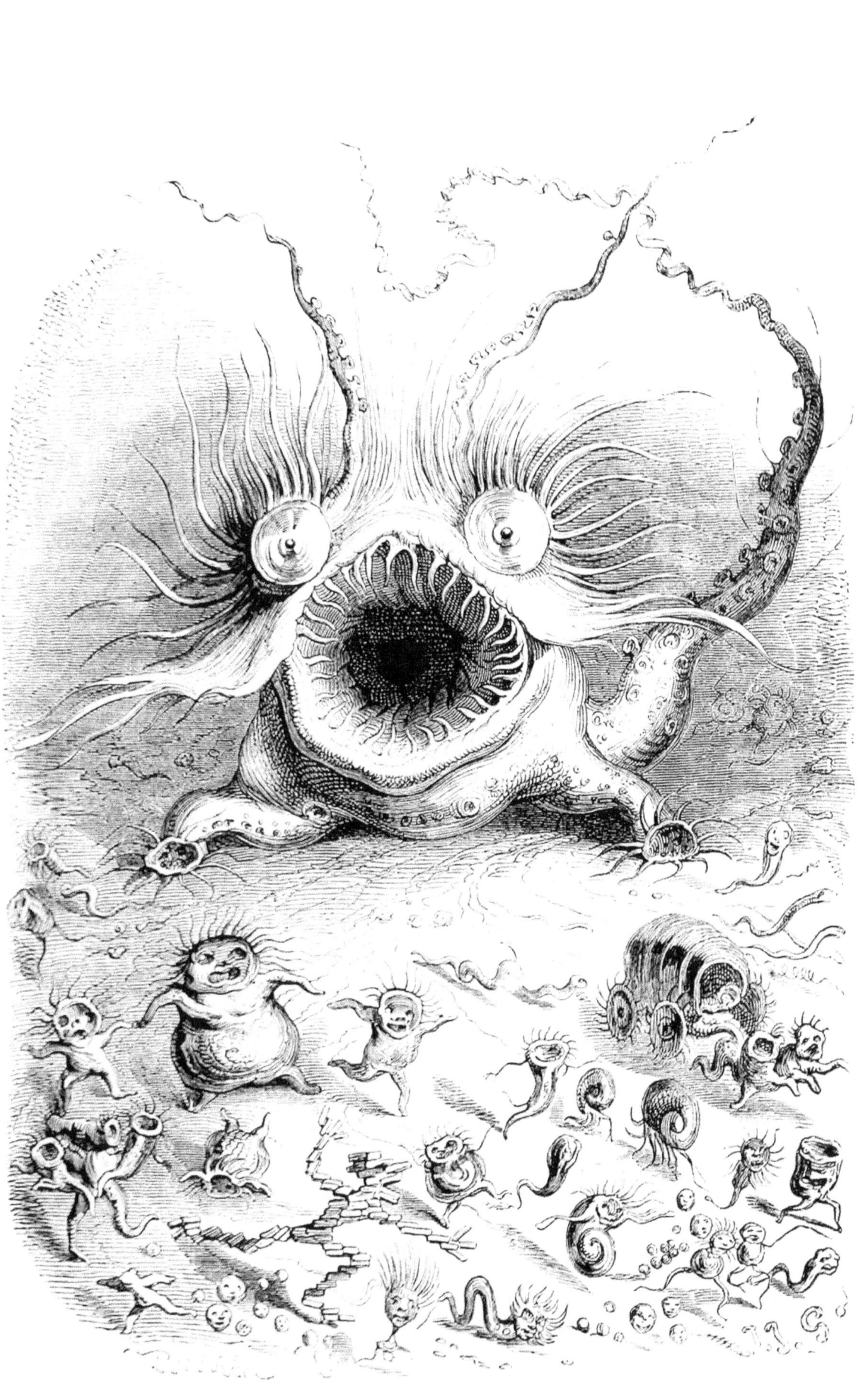

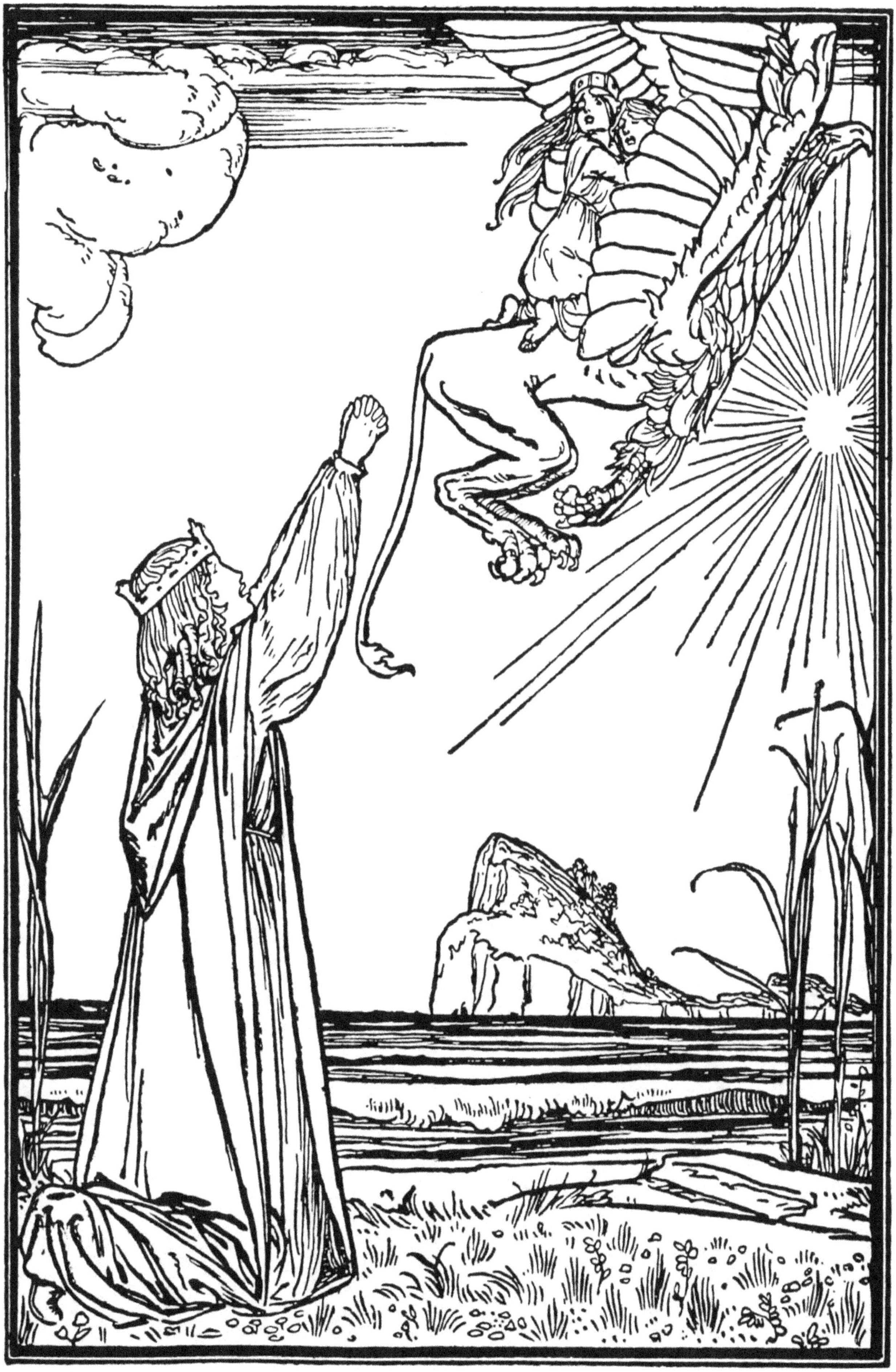

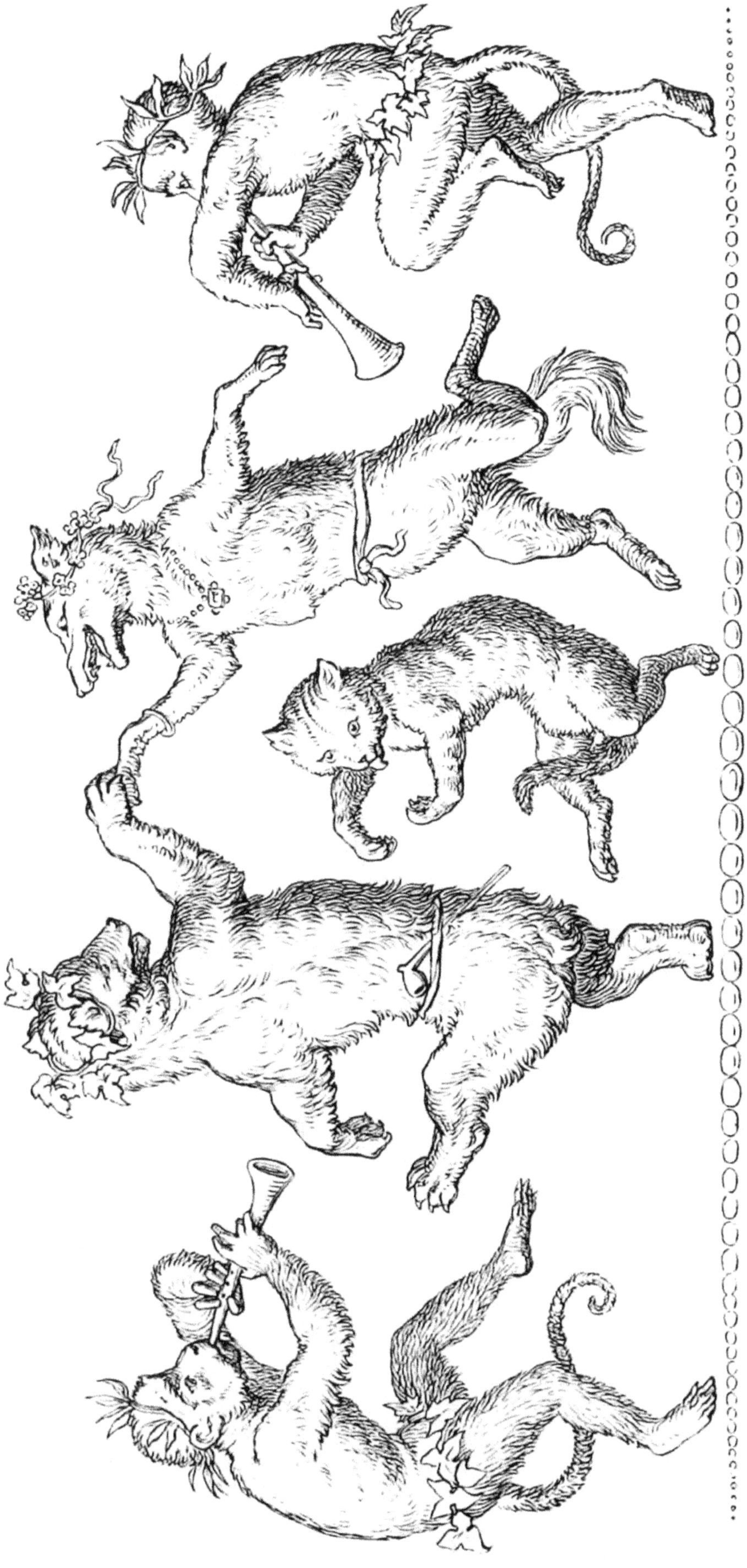